# A Philosophy Guide to Street Art and the Law

# Art and Law



Volumes published in this Brill Research Perspectives title are listed at *brill.com/rpal*

# A Philosophy Guide to Street Art and the Law

*By*

Andrea Baldini

BRILL

LEIDEN | BOSTON

This paperback book edition is simultaneously published as issue 2.3 (2018) of *Art and Law*, DOI:10.1163/24684309-12340005.

Library of Congress Control Number: 2018961914

Typeface for the Latin, Greek, and Cyrillic scripts: "Brill". See and download: brill.com/brill-typeface.

ISBN 978-90-04-39403-2 (paperback)
ISBN 978-90-04-39404-9 (e-book)



This book is printed on acid-free paper and produced in a sustainable manner.

[Doing a graffiti] is basically proving that people have overcome certain fears and constrictions about how they are told to live.

FUEL, DDS Crew

# Contents

# Acknowledgments

While writing this work, I have received inspiration and help from many people. For this, I am deeply grateful. I need to thank few scholars from very different disciplines, who helped me navigate the interdisciplinary difficulties of my project. I am particularly indebted to the precious advices of philosopher Andrea Borghini, who is a very generous listener and critic. I am also grateful to legal scholars Enrico Bonadio and Anjali Vats for their substantial help. My gratitude goes also to Dom Lopes, who encouraged me to write on street art, and to the enthusiastic researchers I met at the Urban Creativity Lisbon Conference. A special thought goes to curator Pietro Rivasi and graffiti writer Fra32. This work could not have been completed in the absence of their support. Fra32 also allowed me to use some of his glorious photographs. I also need to thank the editors of this journal and anonymous reviewers for their insightful comments and suggestions.

# Illustrations

# A Philosophy Guide to Street Art and the Law

*Andrea Baldini*
Nanjing University, China
*andrea.baldini@nju.edu.cn*

## Abstract

What is the relationship between street art and the law? It is argued that street art has a constitutive relationship with the law. A crucial aspect of the identity of this urban art kind depends on its capacity to turn up-side down dominant uses of public spaces. Street artists subvert those laws and social norms that regulate the city. It is shown that street art has not only transformed public spaces and their functions into artistic material, but has also turned its rebellious attitude toward the law into a creative resource. This article aims at elucidating and arguing for this claim, while drawing important implications at the level of street art's metaphysics, value, and relationship with rights of intellectual property, in particular copyright and moral rights. At the other end of the spectrum of contractual art, street art is outlaw art.

## Keywords

street art – graffiti – aesthetics – subversiveness – vandalism – copyright

## Introduction: I Fought the Law, and the Law Swanned

In May 1979, the English punk band The Clash released their EP *The Cost of Living*. The recording included among its tracks the cover of Sonny Curtis's "I Fought the Law." The song tells the story of a young criminal who goes to jail after a series of armed robberies. Its simple lyrics and melody have the incredible power to connect with rebels and non-conformists of different generations. With their louder rendition of the song, The Clash's version became one of the anthems of the punk movement and inspired many to embrace

 | DOI:10.1163/9789004394049_002

alternative life-styles. It also was instrumental in bringing mainstream fame and recognition to punk music.[1]

Recently, the world has seen a rise to popularity of another subcultural art form: street art. Since Banksy's commercial breakthrough in the mid-2000s, this urban art form has conquered the hearts of many art lovers. In 2017, a poll revealed that one of the most iconic pieces of the Bristol artist, *Girl with a Balloon*, had become Britain's favorite artwork, taking the place of Constable's *Hay Wain* in the hearts of Her Majesty's subjects.[2]

The elevation of street art to a popular phenomenon has a somewhat surprising element to it. In effect, one of this art form's recurrent features is street artists' illegal use of urban surfaces as material support for their creations. Much street art is in effect created on private or public property without the owner's consent or authorization. As a consequence of the illegal nature of many of their deeds, street artists are not just masters of color and drawing, but virtuosos of camouflaging, urban climbing, and breaking-in – all skills that make them stand apart from past artists, while also connecting them to an underground world of crime.

In virtually all contexts where street art has picked up momentum, the law has been caught off guard. Legislators, judges, and police officers are often puzzled when dealing with these "crimes of style," as Jeff Ferrell defined graffiti in his pioneering and groundbreaking study.[3] When confronting street art, the law often acts in erratic and contradictory ways: in some occasions, it persecutes its practitioners with technologies and strategies used for fighting against organized crime; in others, it excuses the vandalism of certain street artists in light of the added value that their works bring to the city.[4] The law's casual and desultory way of dealing with this urban artistic practice may suggest the following analogy: the law swans in front of street art, as this introduction's title says.

The general goal of this work is to clarify at least some aspects of the complex relationship between street art and the law. In this sense, it follows in the

---

1 For an interesting discussion of punk, see Erik Hannerz, *Performing Punk* (New York, NY: Palgrave Macmillan, 2015).

2 Maev Kennedy, "Banksy Stencil Soars Past Hay Wain as UK's Favourite Work of Art," *The Guardian*, July 25, 2017, https://www.theguardian.com/artanddesign/2017/jul/26/banksy-balloon-girl-hay-wain-favourite-uk-work-of-art-constable-poll-nation.

3 Jeff Ferrell, *Crimes of Style. Urban Graffiti and the Politics of Criminality* (Boston, MA: Northeastern University Press, 1996).

4 For a discussion of the law's quasi-schizophrenic take on street art, see Andrea Baldini, "Beauty and the Behest: Distinguishing Legal Judgment and Aesthetic Judgment in the Context of 21st Century Street Art and Graffiti," *Rivista Di Estetica* 65 (2017): 91–106, https://doi.org/10.4000/estetica.2161.

footsteps of other prominent scholarly works investigating the link connecting this urban art form with issues of legality and illegality.[5] Previous studies, however, have been carried out within the disciplinary domains of criminology and critical legal studies. The novelty of the present study is to bring the conceptual and theoretical resources developed in various fields of contemporary philosophy to bear on these questions. As far as I know, this is the first work by a philosopher that systematically investigates (the connection between) street art and the law.

Although the present discussion of the relationship between street art and the law develops along lines that are clearly interdisciplinary, the methodology of this work is firmly rooted in conceptual clarification and analysis. However, this aspect should not lead the reader to think that my discussions are inherently abstract and practically irrelevant. To borrow Ronald Dworkin's expression, my philosophical approach works distinctly from the inside out. I start from practical problems and then consider the philosophical issues that are relevant to solve them.

My philosophical perspective draws primarily from debates in Anglo-American philosophy, in particular those recently developed in the subfields of aesthetics and philosophy of art, social ontology, and philosophy of law. I use material from fields such as communication studies, cultural studies, criminology, legal studies, sociology, urban studies, and visual culture as tools for enriching my understanding and historic-contextual knowledge of the practice of street art.

Methodologically, my research also profits from my daily "hanging out" with street artists, street art curators, and street art lovers.[6] Immersing myself at an informal level in the cultural and social experiences of street artists by talking (both online and offline), hearing and sharing stories, and spending considerable amounts of time together with them has been a source of knowledge and insight – even at an existential and personal level. Reaching the vicinity of

5 See, in particular, Ferrell, *Crimes of Style*; Gregory J. Snyder, *Graffiti Lives: Beyond the Tag in New York's Urban Underground* (New York: New York University Press, 2009); Alison Young, *Street Art, Public City: Law, Crime and the Urban Imagination* (Abingdon, Oxon; New York, NY: Routledge, 2014).

6 Clifford Geertz, "Deep Hanging Out," *The New York Review of Books* 45, no. 16 (October 22, 1998): 69–72; Jean Pfaelzar, "Hanging Out: A Research Methodology," *Legacy: A Journal of American Women Writers* 27, no. 1 (2010): 140–159, https://doi.org/10.5250/legacy.27.1.140; Ben Walmsley, "Deep Hanging out in the Arts: An Anthropological Approach to Capturing Cultural Value," *International Journal of Cultural Policy* 24, no. 2 (2018): 272–91, https://doi.org/10.1080/10286632.2016.1153081.

an insider's perspective has considerably shaped my views on street art in general and, of course, on its relationship with the law.

The overall thesis or main idea of this work is, to state it as a slogan, that *street art has a constitutive relationship with the law*. In other words, the very existence of street art, as the art form that it is, depends on its conflictual relationship with the law. Street art has not only transformed public space and its uses into artistic material, but has also turned its (often conflictual) link with the law into an artistic resource. This monograph aims at elucidating and arguing for this claim, while drawing some implications at the level of street art's protection, promotion, and preservation.

Before offering a summary of this essay, I need to add an important qualification, which has to do with the definition of street art that I favor throughout this work. Some of those who write on street art, such as famous art gallerist Magda Danysz, are skeptical about the possibility of street art demarcation. "Street Art," she writes, "is in motion and the simple act of giving it a name, of reducing it to a word or an expression is problematic."[7] And yet, I believe that these worries are misdirected. A working definition of street art is not only useful but necessary whenever we write about cultural phenomena. The only other option is to bring one's pre-critical biases and assumptions to do the definitional work.

Of course, if what we are looking for is an exact and ultimate definition of street art, it may very well be the case that we will never be able to provide one – though certainty would require proof, not a mere doubt. But definitions need not be developed only for this reason. For instance, as Joseph Margolis reasonably points out, by developing a definition of tragedy, Aristotle has not "found the natural joints (the *logically* essential distinctions) of the concept".[8] He has developed a useful definition that "illuminates in a notably arresting way the salient history" of the genre.[9] In defining street art, I opt for this more modest definitional goal.

What the salient histories of art forms are, of course, may very well be contested. However, there are remedies to this problem. A suitable strategy to justify a particular historical narrative that a definition suggests is to opt for a value-centered characterization of the art form under scrutiny. Evaluative definitions of art rely on providing accounts of why individuals value making

7 Magda Danysz, *From Style Writing to Art: A Street Art Anthology* (Roma: DRAGO, 2010), 12.

8 Joseph Margolis, "The Importance of Being Earnest about the Definition and Metaphysics of Art," *The Journal of Aesthetics and Art Criticism* 68, no. 3 (2010): 221, https://doi.org/10.1111/j.1540-6245.2010.01413.x.

9 Margolis, 221.

and appreciating art or, perhaps more appropriately, a specific art form.[10] They differ from classificatory definitions, which are descriptive and aim at accommodating all or most of those things that we intuitively recognize as art – or as examples of an art form. The advantage of evaluative definitions is their capacity to clarify the motivations animating a practice – its embedded values. This in turn provides us with normative traction allowing us to discern between what is salient and what is not in the history of a genre, in spite of what our intuitions could suggest in terms of demarcation. For this reason, I propose here an evaluative definition.

In his recent work on the definition of art, Dominic McIver Lopes develops a theory of art forms or art kinds that places emphasis on matters of value.[11] By drawing on Lopes's general theory of art, I maintain that street art is an art kind or art form. Art kinds are appreciative kinds.[12] Appreciative kinds are groups of particulars that share a common value.[13] We appreciate a particular $p_1$ qua example of a specific appreciative kind $K$ in comparison with arbitrarily any other particular $p_x$ in $K$. Moreover, judgments about the goodness of $p_1$ qua $K$ depends on the essential value characterizing $K$ as an appreciative kind. For instance, an item belongs to the appreciative kind toaster if it is able to toast, and it is a good toaster if it toasts in a comparatively better manner than other items that are also toasters.

What is the value that works of the art kind 'street art' share? In previous work, I have argued that street art is essentially subversive.[14] In other words, its subversiveness, that is, its subversive value, is what street artworks share, and is what makes street art the art kind that it is. It is what drives practitioners and appreciators of street art in doing what they do. Street art's subversiveness

10 A recent strand in philosophy of art has set aside the goal of providing a general definition of art, but has been focusing on definitions of local artistic genres. See, for instance, Dominic McIver Lopes, *Beyond Art* (Oxford: Oxford University Press, 2014).

11 Lopes; Dominic McIver Lopes, *A Philosophy of Computer Art* (New York: Routledge, 2010).

12 Lopes, *Beyond Art*, chap. 7.

13 Lopes, 130; Lopes, *A Philosophy of Computer Art*, 17.

14 Andrea Baldini, "Street Art: A Reply to Riggle," *The Journal of Aesthetics and Art Criticism* 74, no. 2 (2016): 187–91; Andrea Baldini, "Quand les murs de béton muets se transforment en un carnaval de couleur. Le street art comme stratégie de résistance sociale contre le modèle commercial de la visibilité," *Cahiers de Narratologie. Analyse et Théorie Narratives* 30 (2016); Andrea Baldini and Pamela Pietrucci, "Knitting a Community Back Together: Spontaneous Public Art as Citizenship Engagement in Post-Earthquake L'Aquila," in *Territories of Political Participation. Public Art, Urban Design, and Performative Citizenship*, ed. Luigi Musarò and Laura Iannelli (Milan: Mimesis International, 2017), 115–32; Baldini, "Beauty and the Behest"; Andrea Baldini, "Dangerous Liaisons: Graffiti in Da Museum," in *Un(Authorized)//Commissioned*, by Pietro Rivasi and Andrea Baldini (Rome: WholeTrain Press, 2018), 26–32.

is a combination of aesthetic value and political value. It is a function of its capacity to question acceptable uses of public spaces. Street artists challenge dominant spatial politics by appropriating the visible surfaces of the city through the use of colors, shapes, and witty designs that disrupt common assumptions about the appearances of the urban landscape.

By drawing on Martin Irvine's characterization of street art, one could also explain the subversiveness of this art kind in terms of Rancière's notion of the "distribution of the sensible" (*partage du sensible*).[15] The French philosopher introduces this notion in his famous discussion of the relationship between aesthetics and politics. The distribution of the sensible refers, among other things, to all those (formal) laws and (informal) norms regulating visibility in public space. Those laws and norms determine, for instance, what can be seen in the city's streets, squares, and piazzas. Street art turns those regulations upside-down.

Current hierarchies of visibility grant a monopoly over the use of visible surfaces in the city to commercial communication.[16] That is, the urban landscape is inundated with billboards, posters, neon signs, and stickers. Ads occupy a large portion of our visual experience of the city, which has been turned into an oversized advertising hub. When walking down the road, waiting for a bus, commuting by using the subway, we see everywhere campaigns from the latest products that this or the other brand have just released. I have called this particular distribution of the sensible "the corporate regime of visibility" (*le modèle commercial de la visibilité*).[17]

I hasten to add that when talking about the corporate regime of visibility, I am not claiming that corporations have direct control over all urban spaces. Though the rise of privately owned public spaces (POPS) is a growing and alarming phenomenon, it would be inaccurate to say that businesses preside over public spaces.[18] By calling the dominant distribution of the sensible in the

15 Martin Irvine, "The Work on the Street: Street Art and Visual Culture," in *The Handbook of Visual Culture*, ed. Ian Heywood et al. (London: Berg, 2012), 235–78; Jacques Rancière, *Le partage du sensible: esthétique et politique* (La Fabrique éd., 2000).

16 Laura E. Baker, "Public Sites versus Public Sights: The Progressive Response to Outdoor Advertising and the Commercialization of Public Space," *American Quarterly* 59, no. 4 (2007): 1187–1213; Michel de Certeau and Luce Giard, *Culture in the Plural* (Minneapolis: University of Minnesota Press, 1998); Kurt Iveson, "Branded Cities: Outdoor Advertising, Urban Governance, and the Outdoor Media Landscape," *Antipode* 44, no. 1 (2012): 151–74, https://doi.org/10.1111/j.1467-8330.2011.00849.x; Armand Mattelart, *Advertising International: The Privatization of Public Space* (London and New York: Routledge, 1991).

17 Baldini, "Quand les murs de béton muets se transforment en un carnaval de couleur," 5.

18 Timothy Weaver, "The Privatization of Public Space: The New Enclosures," SSRN Scholarly Paper (Rochester, NY: Social Science Research Network, 2014), http://papers.ssrn.com/abstract=2454138.

city 'corporate regime of visibility,' I am suggesting that public space has been turned into a commodity, and that its uses are reduced to economic transactions. For instance, one can certainly find in the city instances of political communication, which are not expressive of economic power but of political authority. However, even political communication follows a business approach to public space and its uses: it adopts the language of commercial advertising and buys access to visible surfaces through a fee. There is a logic of profit that structures exchange in capitalist economy. The corporate regime extends this logic to the way that spaces and their uses are conceptualized in the neoliberal city.

Street art primarily (though not exclusively) challenges the corporate regime of visibility as just discussed.[19] Banksy admits that street art is his weapon of choice against advertising, an idea that resonates sympathetically with the words of other prominent street artists, including Ron English and Shepard Fairey.[20] By hijacking – at no cost for viewers – the walls of our cities, through the use of colorful forms and witty designs which are often filled with irony and satire, street artworks call into question the commodification of our public spaces: the exceptionality of street art resides in transgressing the rules of market economy by being a "gift" to the city.[21] As Michel de Certeau argues, in capitalist economies gifts carry a subversive potential insofar as they challenge the logic of value exchange. In effect, gifts are not traded with the expectation of receiving something in return. For this reason, de Certeau writes, in a profit economy, gift giving "appears as an excess (a waste), a challenge (a rejection of profit), or a crime (an attack on property)," and is therefore perceived as a transgression.[22]

By creating a temporary zone where habitual norms and laws are suspended, street art can 'make strange' the familiar urban landscape, one street at a time.[23] In "Practicing Criticism," Michel Foucault points out that critique is not about saying that the status quo is wrong, but is about "pointing out on [...] what kinds of familiar, unchallenged, unconsidered modes of

19 In different contexts, street art may very well question other hierarchies of visibility. For instance, for a discussion of street art in post-disaster contexts, see Baldini and Pietrucci, "Knitting a Community Back Together."

20 Banksy, *Wall and Piece* (London: Century, 2005), 9; Irvine, "The Work on the Street," 251; Young, *Street Art, Public City*, 28.

21 Michel de Certeau, *The Practice of Everyday Life* (Berkeley and Los Angeles, CA: University of California Press, 1984), 27; Irvine, "The Work on the Street," 252.

22 de Certeau, *The Practice of Everyday Life*, 27.

23 Michel Foucault, "Practicing Criticism," in *Michel Foucault: Politics Philosophy, Culture Interviews and Other Writings 1977–1984*, ed. L. D. Kritzman (New York: Routledge, 1988), 152–156.

thought the practices that we accept rest."[24] One way in which critique can achieve such a goal is by turning the familiar into something strange. This in turn shows contingency of current practices. Street art uses spaces in unexpected and surprising ways. The introduction of such strangeness demonstrates that dominant hierarchies of visibility and current politics of spatial control are far from necessary. Public space need not be reduced to a commodity to be used only for profit under the logic of the market economy, nor its uses limited to those prescribed by the authorities. Once things start to look and function in ways that exceed our previous assumption, as Foucault writes, "transformation becomes both very urgent, very difficult and quite possible."[25] In this sense, street art's aesthetic-political value – its subversiveness – allows us to reimagine alternative ways to manage urban space, which need not be authoritarian nor commodified.

At a historical level, my definition has important implications. It has significant normative traction insofar as it includes and excludes in non-arbitrary ways some practices and genres that some intuitively call or refuse to call street art. In terms of exclusion, my view clearly distinguishes between street art and official public art. In general, examples of public art are officially sanctioned and often locally negotiated with members of the communities of reference. For this reason, public art – though possibly politically significant – is not subversive.[26]

My definition also excludes other art forms of urban art such as "new muralism" and "aerosol art" from counting as street art.[27] These include, among other things, works related to official programs lacking any subversive or confrontational elements.[28] Urban art understood in this sense is not street art insofar as it lacks the essential value connected to that appreciative kind. I hasten to add

24 Foucault, 154.

25 Foucault, 155. For a sympathetic point of view, see also Marieke de Goede, "Carnival of Money. Politics of Dissent in an Era of Globalizing Finance," in *The Global Resistance Reader*, ed. Louise Amoore (London and New York: Routledge, 2005), 379–391.

26 For systematic discussions of official public art, see Andrea Baldini, "Public Art: A Critical Approach." (Temple University Libraries, 2014); Cher Krause Knight, *Public Art: Theory, Practice and Populism* (Malden, MA: Blackwell, 2008); Lambert Zuidervaart, *Art in Public: Politics, Economics, and a Democratic Culture* (New York, NY: Cambridge University Press, 2011).

27 For a sympathetic take on this distinction, see Ulrich Blanché, "Street Art and Related Terms – Discussion and Working Definition," *Street Art and Urban Creativity Scientific Journal* 1 (2015): 32–39.

28 As I will discuss in details in the following chapters, authorities' approval need not imply a lack of subversiveness. It is though true that much art in the public domain sponsored by official programs is not subversive.

that this exclusion does not imply – as it does for some theorists – that these practices have no value or are inferior to street art.[29] Examples of muralism or aerosol art may exemplify other values that differ from street art's subversiveness, but they can be nonetheless something good.

When considering what my definition includes under the conceptual umbrella of street art, one should notice that it embraces a wide variety of artistic styles and genres. From the perspective of a subversiveness-based account of street art, examples of this art kind include a heterogenous set of artworks ranging from graffiti done in the traditional style of writing (tags, throw-ups, and pieces) to examples of yarn bombing, stencil-graffiti, and street sculpture. As an art kind, street art occupies a higher level of the taxonomy with respect to those styles and genres that are all subsumed under the concept 'street art'. In other words, street art stands to graffiti, stencil-graffiti, yarn-bombing, street sculpture, etc. just like literature stands to novel, poetry, short story, etc.

My view does not distinguish between graffiti and street art, as many do, and this point deserves some comment.[30] Such a distinction, I concede, is not without its merit. Yet, I believe, it seems to obscure more than what it illuminates. In particular, it conceals a crucial critical and interpretative claim: Echoing Joe Austin, what is interesting about street art is the same as what is interesting about graffiti – that is, its subversive appropriation of urban public spaces.[31] Writing emerged earlier than representational styles of street art *à la Banksy*, if one can use this expression. Graffiti is then the original form of street art.

Let me add a further thought about the place that graffiti occupies within my account. I do not simply believe that writing is the original form of street art in historical terms, but also in terms of value: Writing is the most radical and uncompromised embodiment of street art. With their undiluted rebellious charge, tags, throw-ups, and pieces embody the subversive value of street art to a level that is seldom found in other genres. In this sense, my account of

29 Among others, Javier Abarca defends the view that muralism lacks in value. See, for instance, Javier Abarca, "From Street Art to Murals: What Have We Lost?," *Street Art and Urban Creativity Scientific Journal* 2, no. 2 (2016): 60–67.

30 For an account that distinguishes graffiti from street art, see Young, *Street Art, Public City*, 4. For a sympathetic view that characterizes graffiti as a form of street art see Pietro Rivasi, "Vandalism as Art: Unauthorized Paintings Vs Institutional Art Shows and Events – the Modena Case Study," in *Un(Authorized)//Commissioned*, by Pietro Rivasi and Andrea Baldini (Rome: Whole Train Press, 2018), 11–15.

31 Joe Austin, *Taking the Train: How Graffiti Art Became an Urban Crisis in New York City* (New York and Chichester, UK: Columbia University Press, 2001).

street art – as well as the discussion of its relationship with the law – is graffiti-centered. Examples of writing are core cases of street art in my account.

I am aware that considering graffiti as street art is an idea that is likely to find opposition (to put it mildly) from many writers. I can hear hordes of them shouting at me: "We are *not* street artists!" In spite of this resistance, I stand my ground. My concern is to reorient current discussions and conceptualizations of street art so that the central role of graffiti is acknowledged – not for partisan reasons, but for philosophical ones. My suspicion is that often writers separate themselves from street artists for the following reason: Much street art – or "fake street art," as Jo Confino calls it – has hijacked the rebellious nature of graffiti in the absence of any street credit, that is, that fame and reputation that is at the very core of writing.[32]

Before moving forward, let me provide my readers with a summary of the text. By following the inside-out approach that my methodology embraces, each one of the three chapters included in this essay addresses a specific question that has been of practical interest for those invested in street art. Each chapter tries to elucidate the assumptions that ground these questions. After a critical review of such assumptions, I will explicitly answer the chapter's question and, within the limits of this essay's length and scope, propose insights for developing new legal trajectories.

The order of the chapters follows a movement from the most basic and abstract philosophical question to more applied issues. Chapter 1 deals with metaphysical concerns about the constitutive relations between street art and the law. Chapter 2 brings the metaphysical discussion of Chapter 1 to bear on the analysis of an evaluative dimension of street art. Chapter 3 uses the discussions of Chapters 1 and 2 to address an applied philosophical question about the relationship between art, market, and the law.

I could not address in the space provided all the issues that emerge as a consequence of the interaction between street art and the law. In particular, this essay largely ignores questions about the relationship between street art, the law, and institutions such as museums. There is no dedicated discussion of this point here, although I have addressed the issue in another publication.[33] Also, the role that street artists' intentions play in shaping the relationship of street art with the law is one theme that I could not examine in detail.

32 Jo Confino, "'Fake Street Art Sucks': Perrier Replaces Williamsburg's Nelson Mandela Mural," *The Guardian*, September 26, 2014, sec. Guardian Sustainable Business, http://www.theguardian.com/sustainable-business/2014/sep/26/fake-street-art-sucks-perrier-replaces-williamsburgs-nelson-mandela-mural-with-huge-advertisement.

33 Pietro Rivasi and Andrea Baldini, *Un(Authorized)//Commissioned* (Rome: Whole Train Press, 2018).

Chapter 1 addresses a question about what Tony Chackal calls street art's illegality condition.[34] Is street art essentially illegal? I suggest that we can interpret this question as asking whether illegality is a necessary or a sufficient condition for an artwork to be street art. I show that illegality is neither one of those things. I argue that illegality is rather a salient and recurrent property of street art. Such a property also grounds street art's subversiveness. In other words, illegality confers subversiveness upon the whole practice of street art.

Chapter 2 examines an issue that has been very popular in discussions of street art: Is it really art, or is it vandalism? I provide different alternative interpretations of the question while developing an analysis of the assumptions implied by it. I show that the binary opposition ('art or vandalism') that this question assumes is false and misleading. By considering the subversive nature of street art that I have discussed in Chapter 1, I argue that street art is both art and vandalism. In clarifying this claim, I suggest that vandalism is a significant artistic technique or tool that street artists use to imbue their creations with meaning. In this sense, street art's artistic significance is a function (among other things) of its vandalism. Its artistic nature as a practice partly but importantly depends on its illegal appropriation of visible surfaces.

Chapter 3 uses the conceptual apparatus developed in Chapters 1 and 2 to address an important applied issue: Should property rights extend to street art? In particular, this chapter focuses on the relationship between street art, copyright, and moral rights. The chapter's goal is to find a moral justification for extending copyright and moral rights to street artworks. I cast doubts on the possibility of finding such a justification. I argue that an extension of copyright and moral rights to street art is likely to jeopardize its subversive nature, and would also introduce fatal distortions into the practice. In spite of my skepticism, I offer a proposal for a legal framework that could suitably protect street art from corporate appropriation.

Finally, in the Conclusion I frame the topic of this volume within the landscape of contemporary art, by arguing that the peculiar nature of street art *qua* art kind rests precisely in its unique and novel constitutive relationship with the law.

---

34 Tony Chackal, "Of Materiality and Meaning: The Illegality Condition in Street Art," *The Journal of Aesthetics and Art Criticism* 74, no. 4 (2016): 359–70, https://doi.org/10.1111/jaac.12325.

## Part 1. Walls, Laws, and Vandals: Is Street Art Essentially Illegal?

### 1 *Introduction*

No one can deny that there is an intimate connection between street art and the law. Street artists are often disparaged as mere vandals ruining public and private properties at the expenses of respectable citizens and law-abiding owners. Since the early 1980s, cities across the globe have developed specific laws against the proliferation of urban markings; they have created squads dedicated to the prosecution of violators and the removal of their deeds. But what is the link binding law and street art together? In particular, is street art necessarily illegal? Or, is illegality a sufficient condition for an artwork to be street art? All of these are metaphysical questions which deal with the nature of street art's identity. In this chapter, I argue that illegality is neither a necessary nor sufficient condition for an artwork to be street art. However, 'being illegal' functions as a ground for the social holistic property of 'being subversive.'

Section 2 provides a formal definition of illegality. I suggest that something is illegal if and only if it violates a positive law according to a judge's decision. Section 3 shows that illegality formally understood cannot be a necessary condition for a work to be a work of street art. Section 4 develops the discussion of the previous section and examines the issue of whether illegality is a sufficient condition for a work to be a work of street art. I claim here that illegality cannot act as such a condition. In section 5, after characterizing subversiveness as a social holistic property, I maintain that illegality is a grounding property of street art's subversiveness.

### 2 *Defining Illegality*

Recent scholarship on street art has acknowledged the constitutive relationship connecting this art kind – with its many related practices – and the law.[35] It characterizes street art in ways that connect the identity of this art kind with

35 See, among others, Sondra Bacharach, "Street Art and Consent," *The British Journal of Aesthetics* 55, no. 4 (2015): 481–95, https://doi.org/10.1093/aesthj/ayv030; Baldini, "Beauty and the Behest"; Blanché, "Street Art and Related Terms – Discussion and Working Definition"; Ulrich Blanché, "Qu'est-ce que le Street art? Essai et discussion des définitions," *Cahiers de Narratologie. Analyse et théorie narratives*, no. 29 (2015), https://doi.org/10.4000/narratologie.7397; Andrea Brighenti, "At the Wall: Graffiti Writers, Urban Territoriality, and the Public Domain," *Space and Culture* 13, no. 3 (2010): 315–32, https://doi.org/10.1177/1206331210365283; Chackal, "Of Materiality and Meaning"; Kurt Iveson, "The Wars on Graffiti and the New Military Urbanism," *City* 14, no. 1–2 (2010): 115–34, https://doi.org/10.1080/13604810903545783; Ferrell, *Crimes of Style*; Young, *Street Art, Public City*.

illegality. In her seminal monograph *Street Art, Public City*, Alison Young identifies illegality as a salient and recurrent feature of street artworks.[36] In a similar vein, Sondra Bacharach writes that works of street art are "often illegal."[37] Tony Chackal, who has dedicated an article to what he calls the illegality condition of street art, claims that street art is prototypically and paradigmatically illegal.[38] In discussing the nature of street art, I myself have suggested that illegality is a resource by means of which street artists and writers imbue their works with subversive power.[39] Put briefly, there is thus a general consensus that the relationship between street art and illegality is not merely accidental.

Still, within this context, what do we mean when we say that street art is 'illegal'? How should we define 'illegality'? We shall call this the *definition question*. Readers might find the question trivial. And yet, as it so happens with many philosophical questions, there is more to this inquiry than meets the eye. In effect, within the academic debate on street art, scholars have been using the notion of illegality in a variety of ways. Possible ambiguity and vagueness can follow from the heterogeneous use of this concept. The goal of this section is to correct such terminological issues by defining illegality precisely enough for the present discussion. As we shall see, the definition that I develop here is also handy in addressing other conceptual issues that arise when considering the relationship between street art and the law.

In her account, Bacharach maintains that "street art has emerged, occupying a metaphysically suspect grey area between illegal activity and bona fide art."[40] An essential feature that makes street art the thing that it is, according to Bacharach, is to be "aconsensually produced."[41] By "aconsensually," she refers to a property of those artworks that are "made without the consent of the property owner on whose property the work exists."[42] The aconsensual nature of street art, Bacharach rightly observes, creates an obvious tension between this practice and the law. As a consequence of such a tension, street artworks "tend to (though *need* not) be illegal."[43]

---

36 Young, *Street Art, Public City*.

37 Bacharach, "Street Art and Consent," 487.

38 Chackal, "Of Materiality and Meaning."

39 Baldini, "Quand les murs de béton muets se transforment en un carnaval de couleur"; Baldini, "Beauty and the Behest"; Baldini and Pietrucci, "Knitting a Community Back Together."

40 Bacharach, "Street Art and Consent," 481.

41 Bacharach, 481.

42 Bacharach, 481.

43 Bacharach, 481.

In her paper, Bacharach does not further explain the relationship between street art and the law. But her use of the term illegal raises at least the following significant conceptual concern: How is it possible for a street artwork to be aconsensually produced and at the same time to be legal? The aconsensual installation of an artwork in the city seems to imply a *de jure* violation of those laws regulating the use of public or private property. Bacharach does not see this complication, and never explicitly answers the previous question, which should require at least some explanation. Her work, then, does not seem to provide us with a sufficiently precise definition of illegality that would be capable of illuminating our discussion. We need to look somewhere else.

In their respective discussions of street art, both Young and Chackal provide us with a more explicit characterization of the notion of illegality than Bacharach. While examining the key features of street art, Young maintains that "the illegality of the work exist[s] either as a result of its placement without permission or through the assumptions about the work brought by the spectator."[44] She is therefore emphasizing a crucial ambiguity that characterizes how general publics connect street artworks and illegality. In effect, in everyday discourse, illegality is often treated either as a formal relationship with the law or as a way in which viewers see and interpret a specific example of street art.

Explicitly drawing on Young's account, Chackal elaborates on this distinction. He claims that "illegality is both a *legal* and *social* status."[45] In the legal sense, a work of street art is illegal when it physically uses the street without permission: illegal works are works that are made although one realizes that he or she is trespassing on private property and, in doing so, has transgressed positive laws. In the social sense, which he also calls "illicitness," a street artwork is illegal insofar as it "transverse dominant customs or traditions."[46] Street art therefore can also be illegal by questioning current ways of using public space, even without violating any positive law.

Young's and Chackal's respective characterizations of illegality illuminate an important aspect of street art, which one could summarize as follows: The antagonistic and rebellious nature of street art can come either from violating positive laws or from challenging dominant traditions and customs.[47] Yet, I hasten to add, their discussion of illegality raises important conceptual issues,

44 Young, *Street Art, Public City*, 8.

45 Chackal, "Of Materiality and Meaning," 362.

46 Chackal, 362. See also Young, *Street Art, Public City*, 4.

47 I also claim something similar. See Baldini, "Street Art: A Reply to Riggle"; Baldini, "Quand les murs de béton muets se transforment en un carnaval de couleur"; Baldini and Pietrucci, "Knitting a Community Back Together."

which have implications that confuse rather than clarify our understanding of the relationship between street art and the law. For this reason, an important correction needs to be made.

To put it in a nutshell, what Chackal calls the 'social sense of illegality' – or 'illicitness' – does not refer to any particular that we can literally call 'illegal.' In other words, illegality exists in the legal sense, but not in the social sense. Viewers' responses – and the assumptions that inform them – certainly do not make a work of street art illegal. Also, challenging dominant customs and traditions need not be enough to make something illegal. Using pineapple and ham as pizza toppings certainly goes against Neapolitan traditions of pizza-making. However, serving Hawaiian pizza – even in Naples – is not enough for you to be sent to jail (although it might be enough to warrant concerns for one's own personal safety).[48] In a non-metaphorical sense, illegality is a *formal* notion that exists only in relationship to the law.

But what do I mean when I say that illegality is a formal notion? Let me briefly clarify this point. I should emphasize that I am not embracing any form of legal formalism. That is, I do not subscribe to the idea that, in answering legal questions, "formal considerations are prior to substantive ones."[49] My discussion here remains neutral about specific approaches to the philosophy of law. Quite to the contrary, I am suggesting something very modest, which even legal pragmatists – arguably at the opposite end of the spectrum in legal theory when compared to formalists – would accept. That is, there are "bound to be formalist pockets" in legal systems of adjudications.[50]

When admitting that there are "formalist pockets" in at least parts of the law, I am claiming that legal judgments are more formalized than judgments in other domains such as the aesthetic, the moral, or the political.[51]

48 For a humorous video about Neapolitans' reactions to Hawaiian pizza, see *Le reazioni dei napoletani alla pizza all'ananas*, accessed May 6, 2018, https://youmedia.fanpage.it/video/ab/WfNoxOSwgwL3Hnux. There are of course cases where calling 'pizza' something that does not conform to legal definitions of pizza or calling a menu item 'penne agli scampi' without specifying that the fish is frozen are illegal actions that could at least produce a fine. Other interesting cases include calling a beverage 'champagne' in Europe, even though it was not produced in the appropriate location. See, for instance, Andrea Borghini, "What Is a Recipe?," *Journal of Agricultural and Environmental Ethics* 28, no. 4 (2015): 719–38; Dany Mitzman, "The Day I Ordered Pizza That 'Doesn't Exist,'" *BBC News*, August 5, 2015, sec. Magazine, https://www.bbc.com/news/magazine-33542392.

49 Ernest J. Weinrib, "Legal Formalism," in *A Companion to Philosophy of Law and Legal Theory* (Malden, MA and Oxford, UK: Wiley-Blackwell, 2010), 329, https://doi.org/10.1002/9781444320114.ch20.

50 Richard A. Posner, "Legal Pragmatism Defended," *University of Chicago Law Review* 71 (2004): 684.

51 Baldini, "Beauty and the Behest," 94–98.

As Joseph Margolis argues, "legal questions concern formal findings of responsibility or liability or guilt with regard to normatively freighted charges drawn up in advance".[52] As Robert Summers claims, the law is formal in many ways.[53] Here, I will focus on two of these ways.

First, legal judgments depend primarily on the decisions of judges. That is to say, they depend on institutionally appointed experts who have generally supreme authority in deciding about legal matters. Judges are appointed through formalized selection procedures.[54] Standardized examinations and evaluative processes follow explicit criteria that do not exist in informal domains. Though experts exist in informal contexts, the procedure of selections is loose and rarely officially acknowledged. For instance, "a fair sample," Lopes writes, "draws aesthetic experts from many walks of life."[55] It would be a profound mistake to assume that only individuals with higher degrees in art related disciplines can claim such a qualification. However, this assumption would be correct if we were thinking about judges.

Second, laws are formal in the following technical sense: They are appropriately complete, definitive, and general.[56] "Each of these formal attributes," Summers maintains, "pertains to the structure [...] of the rule, in contrast to its substantive content as such."[57] For instance, the rule "No vehicles in the park" is formal in the sense just explained.[58] It tells us in a suitably complete, definitive, and general sense that introducing a vehicle in the park is a violation of the law. The formality of such a norm, as Mary Mothersill rightly points out in her discussion of the impossibility of aesthetic laws, provides "criteria for the application of [legal] predicates."[59] Of course, I am not ignoring the fact that the application of non-innocuous legal predicates to action is problematic.[60]

---

52 Joseph Margolis, *Moral Philosophy After 9/11* (University Park, PA: Pennsylvania State University Press, 2004), 49.

53 Robert Summers, "The Formal Character of Law," *The Cambridge Law Journal* 51, no. 2 (1992): 242–62; Robert Summers, "How Law Is Formal and Why It Matters," *Cornell Law Review* 82 (1997): 1165–1229.

54 Summers, "The Formal Character of Law," 245–46, 255.

55 Dominic McIver Lopes, "Aesthetic Experts, Guides to Value," *The Journal of Aesthetics and Art Criticism* 73, no. 3 (2015): 326, https://doi.org/10.1111/jaac.12170.

56 Summers, "How Law Is Formal and Why It Matters," 1167.

57 Summers, "The Formal Character of Law," 246.

58 Summers, 247.

59 Mary Mothersill, "Aesthetic Laws, Principles and Properties: A Response to Eddy Zemach," *The Journal of Aesthetics and Art Criticism* 47, no. 1 (1989): 79, https://doi.org/10.2307/431995.

60 For an instructive discussion of the difficulties in the formulation of legal judgements, see among others Costas Douzinas, Shaun McVeigh, and Ronnie Warrington, "The Alta(e)

There is no algorithm connecting abstract norms to concrete cases. Yet, systems of law provide us with explicit instructions for applying these predicates. We lack such instructions in informal domains.

One of the most important achievements of Wittgenstein's *Philosophical Investigations* is his clarification of the differences in terms of criteria of application between formal and non-formal domains of discourse.[61] In everyday discourse, Wittgenstein observes, we communicate in the absence of such criteria. We do not have exact rules in deciding whether something is a camel or a chair. The edges of these concepts are "blurred."[62] And yet, we are able to talk in a perfectly suitable manner about camels and chairs. In formalized domains such as logic, mathematics, and the law, we decide for special purposes to clarify these boundaries. This, in turn, provides us with criteria of application.

When talking about illegality and illicitness in the context of street art, we have a formal definition for the former, but not for the latter. In other words, in systems of law, we can clearly identify illegal particulars (actions, events, objects, etc.) as violations of the law. As a consequence, we have explicit criteria of application for the predicate 'being illegal.' When considering the predicate 'being illicit,' on the contrary, we do not have such exact criteria: what are the boundaries of traditions and customs? When does an action violate them? There are no clear answers to these questions, not even in principle. Some may recognize Hawaiian pizza as pizza, and (sorry Neapolitans!) there is no principled way to prevent that from happening. The informality of everyday language does not allow for the closing of conceptual boundaries, whereas formalized domains such as the law are grounded on that very possibility.

Hence, I suggest that we understand illegality in the formal sense that I have specified above. So here is my answer to the definition question: Something is illegal if and only if it violates a positive law according to a judge's decision. To put it slightly more formally, in this context, 'being illegal' is a relational property of a work of street art. An artwork, call it *s*, possesses the characteristic relational property of street artworks if and only if *s* bears a specific relation to a legal system *L*, which consists of a set of laws $<l_1, l_2, l_3, \ldots, l_n>$. In particular, *s* violates one or more of the laws in *L*. Such a violation is determined by the evaluation of a judge *J*.

Rs of Law: The Judgement of Legal Aesthetics," *Theory, Culture & Society* 9, no. 4 (1992): 93–117, https://doi.org/10.1177/026327692009004005.

61 Ludwig Wittgenstein, *Philosophical Investigations* (Oxford, UK: Blackwell, 1953), secs. 66–71.

62 Wittgenstein, sec. 71.

Here, I need to add an important qualification about the ontology of street art, which helps to clarify the nature of illegal works of street art. In general, we tend to identify street art with visual art, that is, with discrete objects which possess a certain set of perceptual properties. However, I suggest that, following David Davies' performance-centered ontology of art, we embrace a performance-centered ontology of street art.[63] This ontology sees a street artwork as a performance, that is, as a series of actions. Those are the actions that bear on the appreciation of the work. Call them *generative actions*. In this sense, we appreciate the finished visual artwork insofar as it provides us with "a perspicuous representation of the performance whereby" it was generated, that is, a representation of its generative actions.[64]

Let me clarify why I prefer a performance-centered ontology here. There might be cases – at least in principle – where a street artist *A* does not violate any of the laws $<l_1, l_2, l_3, ..., l_n>$ of the legal system *L* in, for instance, painting a street artwork *s* in a certain place *p*.[65] However, *A* might be breaking the law in climbing a series of fences in order to reach *p*. If one understands *s* in object-centered terms, then *s* does not seem to be illegal. What is illegal, in effect, is the specific act of trespassing, which seems irrelevant to the identity of *s* thus conceived. However, this seems to clash with the ways in which we generally conceptualize street artwork (fig. 1).

In traditional painting (or other visual artforms), how an artist reached the artwork's location is irrelevant in most cases. But quite the opposite holds in the context of street art. In our example, the act of climbing a fence seems constitutive of *s* just like – let's say – the action of spray-painting its outline. In other words, climbing the fence is an action that bears on our appreciation of the street artwork. There is something about its meaning that one will not appreciate while ignoring these aspects of the generative performance.

Works of street art are generally created in locations that are dangerous or hard to reach. Writers have an ad hoc term to refer to the most extreme spots such as rooftops and freeway signs: They call them "heaven spots" or

63 I defend a performance-center ontology of street art and graffiti in "Dangerous Liaisons: Graffiti in Da Museum," section 4.

64 David Davies, *Art as Performance* (Malden, MA and Oxford, UK: Blackwell, 2004), 116.

65 Here is a possible scenario that exemplifies a case where we only have a violation in accessing a space, rather than in creating a street artwork. Imagine a park where there is a wall – a Hall of Fame – where authorities have granted the possibility to freely paint graffiti. However, the park is open from 9am to 5pm. If one enters the park at 3am in order to paint a graffiti on the Hall of Fame, the only violation of the law will arguably be about trespassing and not spray-painting the graffiti.

FIGURE 1 Climbing a train yard fence
*Note*: For ethical reasons, I intentionally withhold sensitive information about photographs.
PHOTOGRAPH COURTESY OF FRA32

simply "*heavens*" (fig. 2).[66] When looking at street artworks, one imaginatively reconstruct the actions that street artists had to perform in order to access their locations: for example, how one entered a train yard, accessed a rooftop, climbed a billboard, or reached a canal wall. Given the very nature of these locations, these actions are not left in obscurity, but are (imaginatively) obvious to anyone observing these works.[67] This imaginative experience bears on the appreciation of street art. "People look at an oil painting," Banksy writes, "and admire the use of brushstrokes to convey meaning. People look at a graffiti painting and admire the use of a drainpipe to gain access."[68] By opting for a performance-centered ontology, we can broaden the conditions

66 "The Words: Graffiti Glossary," accessed June 22, 2016, https://www.graffiti.org/faq/graffiti.glossary.html.

67 Of course, one can always be wrong about how an artist reached a spot. For instance, one could come to know that an artist reached what appears to be a heaven spot through the use of a crane because the piece was authorized. However, the possibility of being wrong about the generative performance does not suffice as a rebuttal of my view.

68 Banksy, *Wall and Piece*, 237. See also Chackal, "Of Materiality and Meaning," 365.

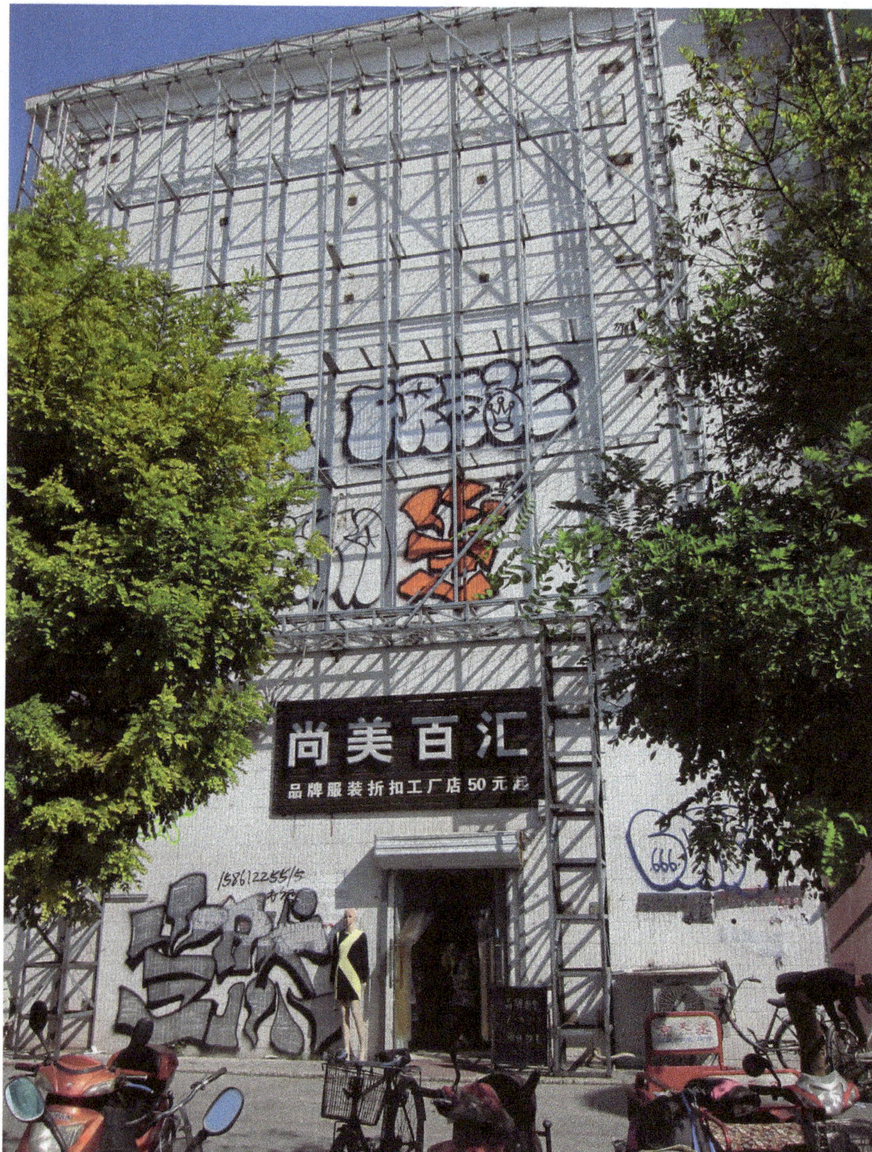


FIGURE 2 Heavens in Beijing
PHOTOGRAPH COURTESY OF FRA32

that can warrant considering a street artwork as illegal, thus accommodating the widely shared intuition that Banksy's quote expresses so well.

Therefore, illegal works of street art – ontologically understood in the performative sense – are those whose generative actions violate codified norms, in particular, norms that usually regulate the use of private and public properties. In the following section, I will discuss the issue of whether street art is necessarily illegal in the sense just specified.

## 3 *Is Street Art Necessarily Illegal?*

One could interpret the claim that street art is essentially illegal in at least two senses. In the first sense, possessing the property of 'being illegal' is a necessary condition for an artwork to be street art. If it is a necessary condition, illegality must be present in *all* genuine examples of street art. In the second sense, one may intend instead that the property of 'being illegal' is a sufficient condition for an artwork to be street art. As a sufficient condition, illegality need not be present in all genuine cases of street art, but it provides us with enough ground for considering an artwork street art. In this section, I discuss the first sense in which one can interpret the claim about the essential relationship between street art and illegality. Is illegality a necessary condition for street art? I argue that this is not the case. I will consider the issue of illegality as a sufficient condition in the following section.

Some among both scholars and practitioners seem to endorse this view. For instance, Joe Austin's view could be plausibly understood as claiming that being illegal is a necessary condition for street art. In "More to See than a Canvas in a White Cube," he criticizes views that see graffiti as an urban problem.[69] Turning this common viewpoint on its head, he argues that "graffiti art is a potential *enhancement* to everyday urban life."[70] In line with what many theorists have suggested, he sees graffiti's positivity as a function of its capacity to bring "disruption of the unexamined assumptions connecting urban visual culture and the existing social order."[71] For Austin, street art has embraced the spirit of graffiti; they both function in similar ways. And such an artform, he believes, is "produced illegally in the shared public spaces of the modern city."[72]

---

69 Joe Austin, "More to See than a Canvas in a White Cube: For an Art in the Streets," *City* 14, no. 1–2 (2010): 33–47, https://doi.org/10.1080/13604810903529142.

70 Austin, 34.

71 Austin, 33. For sympathetic views, see, among others, Baldini, "Street Art: A Reply to Riggle"; Baldini, "Quand les murs de béton muets se transforment en un carnaval de couleur"; Baldini and Pietrucci, "Knitting a Community Back Together"; Kurt Iveson, *Publics and the City* (Malden, MA and Oxford, UK: Blackwell Publishing, 2007); Iveson, "The Wars on Graffiti and the New Military Urbanism"; Cameron McAuliffe and Kurt Iveson, "Art and Crime (and Other Things Besides …): Conceptualising Graffiti in the City," *Geography Compass* 5, no. 3 (2011): 128–43, https://doi.org/10.1111/j.1749-8198.2011.00414.x; Theo Kindynis, "Bomb Alert: Graffiti Writing and Urban Space in London," *The British Journal of Criminology* 58, no. 3 (2018), https://doi.org/doi:10.1093/bjc/azx040.

72 Austin, "More to See than a Canvas in a White Cube," 34.

Among practitioners, the view that street art is necessarily illegal is widespread, in particular among graffiti writers (the most radical among practitioners of street art).[73] In reporting his interview with graffiti writer KATO, Andrea Mubi Brighenti summarizes KATO's view as follows: "writing makes sense only if it remains illegal."[74] Recently, London graffiti legend OKER has made some remarks that seem to advocate the view that illegality is a necessary condition for street art. In commenting on "retired" writers who made their comebacks in a Hall of Fame (a term that today refers to legal walls of graffiti), he claims: "Even if you have consistently done Halls of Fame for the last 20 years, it's irrelevant; it doesn't really matter because what you're doing isn't writing. I'm a writer, when I paint Halls of Fame I consider that 'aerosol art'; it's not graffiti."[75] For these writers, it seems that legal pieces are not street art.

Several scholars challenge this view, and reject the claim that street art is necessarily illegal. I have already mentioned Bacharach, who claims that, though it may often violate positive laws, street art need not be illegal.[76] Unfortunately, she mentions this passingly, without much explanation of why this is the case. Besides Bacharach, it is worthwhile to mention two other perspectives, offering more explicit reasons of why street art need not be illegal. Both arguments are similar as they rely on the strategy of the counterexample. In other words, they appeal to cases that many intuitively recognize as part of a term's reference *and* contradict a definition of such term.

In his ethnographic observations, Brighenti finds that, though "illegality represents the *zero degree* of the practice of writing," writers very often carry out their activities in legal ways by painting walls of Halls of Fame or participating in festivals.[77] In this sense, while providing a benchmark for evaluating the activity of authentic writers, in opposition to those who do "aerosol art," as OKER would say, illegality is not always a property associated with graffiti and street art.

---

73 As I clarify in the Introduction, contrary to some, I consider graffiti the quintessential expression of street art, and not a separate genre. In this respect, I agree with Austin, who believes that what is distinctive and valuable about street art in general is primarily what is valuable about graffiti.

74 Brighenti, "At the Wall," 320.

75 "EXCLUSIVE: Speaking to ... OKER," *Wavey Garms*, accessed May 10, 2018, https://waveygarms.com/blogs/news/speaking-to-oker.

76 Bacharach, "Street Art and Consent," 481.

77 Brighenti, "At the Wall," 318. See also Andrea Brighenti, "Graffiti, Street Art and the Divergent Synthesis of Place Valorisation in Contemporary Urbanism," in *Routledge Handbook of Graffiti and Street Art*, ed. Jeffrey Ian Ross (New York: Routledge, 2016), 158–67.

Young offers a similar argument to Brighenti's. "Invoking the illegality of an image as a central definitional feature," she writes, "is also problematic. Some street artworks are created without permission; others are created with the consent of the property owner."[78] By drawing explicitly on Young's view, Chackal also makes the following claim: "The inclination to keep street art conceptually distinct from public or mainstream art might lead one to think that illegality is a necessary condition of all street art. Yet, as Alison Young notes, positing illegality as a necessary condition is problematic because works seen as paradigmatic are sometimes legal".[79]

From a conceptual point of view, the strategy of the counterexample that both arguments adopt seldom provides sufficient grounds for rejecting a definition. This is particularly the case when dealing with novel and non-mainstream art kinds such as street art. In effect, one could simply deny that the counterexample genuinely belongs to the term's reference in the first place. Linguistic intuitions widely differ among speakers, and – perhaps more importantly – they need not have philosophical relevance. Theories and definitions surely must significantly connect with our ways of speaking and thinking about the world, but they may sometimes diverge from linguistic uses.

By applying this assessment of the strategy of the counterexample to our case, one could simply reject that all the cases that Brighenti, Chackal, and Young have in mind are genuine examples of street art to begin with. Not everything that a poet writes is a poem, one could say. Similarly, not everything that a street artist does qualifies necessarily as street art. Arguably, OKER's remarks are consistent with a view that excludes all these cases as street art, and categorizes them rather as aerosol art or mere urban decoration. The counterexamples given here thus seem to lose their argumentative force.

However, considering the empirical evidence that these arguments bring to the table, I believe that we need a more robust argument if we are to reject the view that street art is necessarily illegal. In the remainder of this section, I will make just such an argument. The argument, as we shall see, relies on the specific understanding of illegality that I have laid out in the previous section, and is grounded on how current systems of law generally operate.

Imagine the following case. Street artist *A* creates street artwork *s* on a train cart *t* without authorization. So far, *s* seems illegal. Police officer *P* walks by *t* just right after *A* has completed *s* and arrests *A*. The day after, *A* appears in

78 Young, *Street Art, Public City*, 4.
79 Chackal, "Of Materiality and Meaning," 361.

court in front of judge *J*. Now, let's assume that – for whatever reason – *J* acquits *A*, thus making *de jure* artwork *s* legal.

If one accepts that street artworks are necessarily illegal, the above imaginary examples has a significant implication. Such an implication, I believe, provides a sufficient ground for rejecting that 'being illegal' is a necessary condition for an artwork to be street art. Since illegality is a formal notion that only judges can adjudicate, then issues of demarcation in street art are necessarily a legal matters. In other words, legal judges would be those who decide whether a particular artwork is a street artwork or mere aerosol art. But the idea that judges have this power seems a *reductio ad absurdum* of the view that street art is necessarily illegal.[80]

Let me make explicit why I believe that judges determining demarcation in street art is an absurd implication that warrants the rejection of the view that 'being illegal' is a necessary condition for street art. In general, we believe that demarcation within art kinds – that is, distinguishing between those particulars who are instances of an art form and those particulars that are not – is negotiated internally to the practice. In other words, whether something is a musical work – to the extent that this classification can be contested – largely depends on considerations emerging from within the practice of music, that is, from the actions and views of (say) composers, conductors, music critics, music players, and concert-goers. Here, for instance, professional opinions from medical doctors about whether some kind of music might be harmful to one's hearing do not have any effect on its demarcation as music. Harmful music can still be music. It would be absurd to think otherwise.

A similar argument holds for street art: Whether something is street art or not – as contested as it could be – is arguably a function of how those involved in the practice at different levels (street artists, street art lovers, street art theorists, etc.) understand the demarcation of the genre. As Kurt Iveson convincingly shows, as a consequence of street art's peculiar nature and its significant relationship with the law, one can surely admit that judges' opinions can profoundly influence the practice and, one could add, its demarcation.[81] What seems implausible is that judges are the ultimate authority in determining whether something is street art. I am sure that even the most radical writers would reject this idea. (They would probably be the first to do so!) Judges are not – and should not be – *arbitri elegantiae* of street art.

80 I need to thank Andrea Borghini, who suggested this point to me.

81 Iveson, "The Wars on Graffiti and the New Military Urbanism."

By highlighting this absurd implication about street art demarcation, I have showed that street art need not be illegal.[82] In the following section, I will consider the issue of whether illegality is a sufficient condition for street art.

## 4 *Is Illegality a Sufficient Condition for Street Art?*

Another possible interpretation of the claim that street art is essentially illegal understands 'being illegal' as a sufficient condition for an artwork to be street art. A sufficient condition for some state of affairs *S* is a condition that, when satisfied, guarantees that *S* obtains. In this context, to say that illegality is a sufficient condition for an artwork to be street art, we mean that given a certain artwork *w*, if *w* is illegal, then *w* is street art.

In order to make the claim plausible, of course, we need to understand artwork here in a certain sense, adding one or more (necessary) conditions. One should think that, in order to qualify as street art, *w* must be made in a certain style, which is one of the styles that are generally associated with street art such as spray paint graffiti (tags, throw-ups, and burners), stencil-graffiti, street sculpture and installation, yarn-bombing, wheat pasted poster art, or sticker art.[83] One could also add that *w* must be installed in a public space of some sort. Depending on one's preferences, the list of additional requirements may vary in its specificity.

Here, I am interested in understanding whether, once we agree on the features that *w* must possess to be considered street art, 'being illegal' is a condition that guarantees that *w* is street art – given that there might be cases of street art that are legal. Within the literature on street art, it seems that scholars have not yet explicitly or systematically explored this possibility. The aim of this section is just to accomplish this very goal. As anticipated, as we shall see, I believe that 'being illegal' is also not a sufficient condition for street art. This discussion will further illuminate my account of the relationship between art and the law, and will be our foundation for developing the next section, where I clarify how we should correctly characterize this relationship.

82 One could wonder whether a street artist's intention of breaking the law is a necessary condition for street art, or how possible changes in the law could affect the identity of street art. Though these concerns are important, I reserve to another time their discussion.

83 Here, I use 'style' as an explanatory notion. In this sense, style is a "shorthand for a set of characteristics which we and those who share our outlook find particularly interesting, arresting, innovatory" in a particular set of works (Richard Wollheim, *Painting as an Art* (Princeton: Princeton University Press, 1987), 26). For a general discussion of style, see Aaron Meskin, "Style," in *Routledge Companion to Aesthetics*, ed. Berys Gaut and Dominic McIver Lopes, 3rd ed. (London: Routledge, 2013), 442–51.

The claim that illegality is a sufficient condition for an artwork to be street art surely possesses *prima facie* plausibility. Perhaps what Brighenti says about illegal artworks being the "zero degree" of the practice of writing could be interpreted as asserting something along this line. In other words, there are many borderline cases – legal artworks, commissioned artworks, etc. – whose identity as street artworks is contested. However, there are some core cases – illegal artworks – that straightforwardly qualify as genuine street art. Their illegality is sufficient for making them street art.

In spite of its plausibility, I believe that the view sketched above is actually false: there are cases of artworks that, although illegal, do not qualify as street art. As a way to provide evidence for this claim, consider the following example. In 2008, the streets of Toronto were suddenly occupied by a series of 324 seven-foot-tall wheat paste posters made in "photograffiti style." The posters presented young males dressed in various street (hipster) styles with a Vespa handlebar instead of their heads. As a consequence of the representational content of these works, many started to call the series *Vespa Squareheads*. Street art communities of practitioners and aficionados immediately recognized Fauxreel as the author of those posters. Fauxreel, whose real name is Dan Bergeron, is a Canadian street artist. His distinctive photographic style gave him a reputation among communities of street art lovers.

Soon after Fauxreel's *Squareheads* appeared on the walls of Toronto, the truth about this series of wheat paste posters emerged. The photograffiti portraits of these mechanical hybrids were actually part of an ad campaign sponsored by Vespa. As an aggressive attempt to promote their new scooter, the Italian brand commissioned Fauxreel to develop their marketing campaign – which also appeared in other Canadian cities such as Vancouver, Calgary, and Montreal. Noticeably, the campaign was *illegal*. That is, the *Squareheads* were installed without consent. Though no "immediate brand recognition" was possible just by looking at the posters of these man-scooter hipsters, stopping by a Vespa dealer in the area would have revealed the mystery.[84]

When the news spread that the *Squareheads* were part of a Vespa's marketing campaign, local audiences responded with interesting reactions. In general, among street art lovers, the commercial nature of Fauxreel's project caused a backlash, and many were vocal in refusing to consider those posters to be examples of street art.[85] In a comment to an internet post, Matthew Nelson,

84 Patricia Simoes, "Vespa Ads Not Cool," *Spacing Toronto* (blog), accessed May 30, 2015, http://spacing.ca/toronto/2008/04/30/vespa-ads-not-cool/.

85 Hrag Vartanian, "Street Art Politics & Commercialization ... How Far Is Too Far?," *Hyperallergic*, accessed May 30, 2015, http://hyperallergic.com/3415/street-art-politics

a local resident of Vancouver, writes: "I can tell you first handedly that this [the *Vespa Squareheads* installation] went over very badly in Vancouver (my home), and within a few short days almost every wheat pasted image was capped, reworked or destroyed."[86] Interestingly enough, as a consequence of what appeared as a commercial sell-out, some started to even question the status of Fauxreel's previous works.

Here is the lesson that we can learn from this episode. We have here a group of artworks that visually and stylistically resembled Fauxreel's regular production. They are also installed in places that are traditionally associated with the production of street artworks. In this sense, we have perfect candidates for street art: The *Vespa Squareheads* seem to satisfy those initial constraints that generally ground the possibility of categorizing an artwork as street art, and were also illegal.

If 'being illegal' was a sufficient condition for an artwork possessing certain formal, stylistic, and locational properties to be street art, then Fauxreel's *Squareheads* should qualify as genuine street artworks. However, this is not the case. Many street art lovers refuse to consider these posters to be street art. Interestingly enough, street art communities embrace the rest of Fauxreel's production, which is also often illegal, as street art. Here is the conundrum: On the one hand, we have Fauxreell's regular production, that is, wheat posters realized in an urban style and installed illegally in a public space, which is widely accepted as street art. On the other hand, we have the *Vespa Squareheads*, which are stylistically indistinguishable from Fauxreel's regular works, illegally installed in the urban landscape, and yet are not accepted as street art. Being illegal, it seems, cannot possibly be a sufficient condition for an artwork to be street art.

At this point, readers may very well ask themselves the following question: Why are Fauxreel's *Vespa Squareheads* not street art? The answer to this question will help us not only understand more clearly the nature of street art, but also – as we shall see in the following section – the specific nature of the relationship between street art and the law. In the remainder of this section, I will provide an answer to that question.

In a nutshell, the commercial nature of Fauxreel's *Vespa Squareheads* is what precludes these posters from being categorized as street art. An argument for this claim could run as follows. As many theorists recognize, with their rebellious intrusion within the urban landscape, street artworks hijack (albeit

-commercialization/; "Vespa Murketing Inspires Fauxreel Backlash?," accessed May 30, 2015, http://www.murketing.com/journal/?p=1310.

86 "Vespa Murketing Inspires Fauxreel Backlash?".

momentarily) the modern city's public spaces and essentially question their acceptable uses and functions.[87] I call this capacity of turning upside-down dominant hierarchies of spatial politics the *subversiveness* of street art.[88] As I have explained in the Introduction, subversiveness is an aesthetic-political value showing that the appreciation of street art transcends the boundaries of the aesthetic domain narrowly construed.[89] Street art as an art kind possesses in effect broad cultural and social significance, and therefore its meaning has larger cultural and social implications.

In general, most of the acceptable uses and functions of today's public spaces are of a commercial nature. Recent scholarship on public space in sociology, urban studies, geography, and economics provides us with ample empirical evidence in favor of the claim that commercial communication has a monopoly over the use of visible surfaces in global metropolises.[90] With billboards, posters, and neon signs, advertising has turned our streets and squares into branded hubs. As Martin Irvine convincingly argues, street art develops a "counter-imagery" that challenges corporate control over urban visibility. In this sense, often (though not always), street art's essential subversiveness has to do with fighting against commercial communication.[91]

---

87 Scholarly works that discuss street art as subversive in the sense that I have specified include, among others, Bacharach, "Street Art and Consent"; Sondra Bacharach, "Finding Your Voice in the Streets: Street Art and Epistemic Injustice," *The Monist* 101, no. 1 (2018): 31–43, https://doi.org/10.1093/monist/onx033; Chackal, "Of Materiality and Meaning"; McAuliffe and Iveson, "Art and Crime (and Other Things Besides ...)"; Iveson, *Publics and the City*; Kurt Iveson, "Cities within the City: Do-It-Yourself Urbanism and the Right to the City," *International Journal of Urban and Regional Research* 37, no. 3 (2013): 941–56, https://doi.org/10.1111/1468-2427.12053; Young, *Street Art, Public City*; Kindynis, "Bomb Alert."

88 Baldini, "Street Art: A Reply to Riggle." See also the Introduction to this volume.

89 Lopes's more inclusive notion of the aesthetic is not narrow, and could accommodate subversiveness as aesthetic value. See Dominic McIver Lopes, "The Myth of (Non-Aesthetic) Artistic Value," *The Philosophical Quarterly* 61, no. 244 (2011): 518–36, https://doi.org/10.1111/j.1467-9213.2011.700.x; Lopes, *Beyond Art*, chap. 5.

90 For a sample of the literature on the growing commercialization of public space, see, among others, Baker, "Public Sites versus Public Sights"; Bradley R. Barnes et al., "Exploring Cosmetics Advertising in Southern China," *International Journal of Advertising* 28, no. 2 (2009): 369–93, https://doi.org/10.2501/S0265048709200606; Iveson, "Branded Cities"; Mattelart, *Advertising International*; Tomas A. Lopez-Pumarejo and Myles Bassell, "The Renaissance of Outdoor Advertising: From Harlem to Hong Kong," *American Journal of Business* 24, no. 2 (2009): 33–40, https://doi.org/10.1108/19355181200900009.

91 In replying to my critique to his view, Riggle suggests that street art does not always challenge commercial communication. See Nicholas Alden Riggle, "Using the Street for Art: A Reply to Baldini," *The Journal of Aesthetics and Art Criticism* 74, no. 2 (2016): 191–95, https://doi.org/10.1111/jaac.12280. However, I have never claimed that: I pointed out that street art *primarily* defies advertising, though it need not to. In Baldini and Pietrucci,

Though illegal, Fauxreel's *Vespa Squareheads* fails to be subversive in the sense just explained. In effect, these wheat-posters do not question dominant uses and functions of public spaces in modern cities. To the contrary, they reinforce such uses and functions, and reaffirm the hegemony of corporate control over our daily lives and the everyday appearance of the urban landscape. One could also add that Fauxreel's *Vespa Squareheads* hijack tactics of dissent against neo-liberal ideologies and politics, and turn them into instruments of corporate profit. As we have seen for many other counter-cultural movements such as punk, rap, and hip-hop, corporations are very skilled at absorbing and devouring movements of dissent. That is exactly what happened with Fauxreel's *Vespa Squareheads*. They clearly show why illegality is not a sufficient condition for an artwork to be street art. In the following section, I use the notion of subversiveness to clarify the nature of the relationship between street art and the law.

## 5 *Illegality as a Ground for Subversiveness*

In the previous sections, after developing a formal definition of illegality, I showed that 'being illegal' is neither a necessary nor a sufficient condition for an artwork to be street art. I have highlighted an absurd implication of the view that illegality is a necessary condition for an artwork to be street art. In particular, such a claim would grant legal judges supreme authority in matters of street art demarcation. When considering the hypothesis that illegality is a sufficient condition for street art, I have pointed out that illegality need not be enough to guarantee that a certain artwork is street art. So, how can we correctly understand the relationship between street art and the law?

Before answering this question, let me quickly turn back to the characterization of street art that I offered earlier in this chapter. As I discussed in the Introduction, one plausible way to understand street art is to consider it as a subversive art kind. The subversiveness of street art, I have suggested, is a function of its capacity to challenge and call into question dominant uses of public spaces in contemporary global metropolises. Many scholars agree on this point, and essentially link the rebellious side of street art with its very nature.[92]

---

"Knitting a Community Back Together: Spontaneous Public Art as Citizenship Engagement in Post-Earthquake L'Aquila," we provide a discussion that is also a reply to Riggle's criticism.

92 Bacharach, "Street Art and Consent"; Bacharach, "Finding Your Voice in the Streets"; Chackal, "Of Materiality and Meaning"; McAuliffe and Iveson, "Art and Crime (and Other Things Besides ...)"; Iveson, "Cities within the City"; Iveson, *Publics and the City*; Ferrell, *Crimes of Style*; Young, *Street Art, Public City*; Kindynis, "Bomb Alert"; Irvine, "The Work

But exactly what kind of property is subversiveness? I suggest that we do *not* understand subversiveness as a property of particular artworks considered in isolation from one another, that is, it is not a feature that pertains to solitary acts of creative expression in the city. Isolated actions, events, and their outcomes are hardly capable of subverting – even momentarily – established orders, hierarchies, and institutions. They are generally perceived as juvenile and unsophisticated gestures, which are mere nuisances rather than actions with political significance.

In the case of street art, subversiveness seems to me a *global property* of the practice taken as a whole. I draw the sense of global that I use here from works in philosophy of science. In general, global properties identify higher order properties of wholes that cannot be reduce to lower level properties of their parts. Global properties are therefore also emergent.[93] Here, I say that subversiveness is a global property of street art insofar as it cannot be reduced to any property (or few properties) shared by all street artworks. Subversiveness is emergent in a distinctly constructivist sense: As we shall see, it depends constitutively on social conferral.[94]

When I talk about the practice of street art, I intend the full range of activities, influences, materials, events, discussions, traditions, customs, tools, skills, and techniques that are connected to the production of street artworks as elements of street art as an art kind. The practice of street art, in other words, includes the "nexus of activities and judgments" that are significantly connected to what street artists do and street art lovers appreciate.[95] In this sense, the practice of street art includes more than the physical gesture of making street artworks. This practice is broader than that, and also includes larger contextual, cultural, historical, political, sociological, and existential aspects. Subversiveness is something connected with this larger sense of the practice of street art here.

More explicitly, I suggest that we consider 'subversiveness' as a *social holistic property* of the practice of street art. Let me explain step-by-step what

---

on the Street"; Baldini, "Street Art: A Reply to Riggle"; Baldini, "Quand les murs de béton muets se transforment en un carnaval de couleur."

93 Paul Humphreys, "Emergence, Not Supervenience," *Philosophy of Science* 64, no. 4 (1997): S337 S345; Paul Humphreys, *Emergence* (Oxford: Oxford University Press, 2016). For an introduction to emergence, see Timothy O'Connor and Hong Yu Wong, "Emergent Properties," in *The Stanford Encyclopedia of Philosophy* (Summer 2015 Edition), ed. Edward N. Zalta, https://plato.stanford.edu/archives/sum2015/entries/properties-emergent/.

94 Borghini, "What Is a Recipe?," 726–28.

95 Peter Lamarque, *The Philosophy of Literature* (Malden, MA: Blackwell, 2009), 7. See also Lopes, *Beyond Art*, chap. 8.

I intend with this expression. Subversiveness is a social property in the sense in which Ásta Sveinsdóttir talks about social properties.[96] By offering a weaker and less demanding account of social properties than, for instance, John Searle or other philosophers dealing with social ontology, Sveinsdóttir understands such properties as "conferred properties."[97] Conferred properties are response-dependent properties. They are attributed to a particular as a result of (some group of) people's dispositions. Specifically, these dispositions are a function of how (some group of) people tend "to behave in certain ways and not others in counterfactual situations."[98]

Sveinsdóttir's account has two positive implications in explaining street art's subversiveness. First, it treats social properties not as simply tracking some physical facts about the world. She believes that social properties are grounded in judgments about these facts. For their part, these judgements create new and interesting social facts.[99] In our case, recognizing subversiveness would not merely amount to recognizing that, for instance, particular street artworks possess certain properties, such as being in a particular style, being installed in a public space, having a particular content, being illegal, etc. Conferring subversiveness instead requires a judgment about these particular facts.

Second, her conferralist account is distinctly context-dependent. In discussing how gender is a property conferred to individuals, Sveinsdóttir writes: "my own suggestion as to how gender is conferred makes gender be highly context-dependent, and the *grounding property or properties* vary with context."[100] In other words, those features that are considered relevant for assigning a specific gender to a person such as "sex assignment, role in biological reproduction, sexual role, role in societal organization, and so on" may very well vary across different historical, geographical, and social contexts.[101]

Similarly, I suggest that subversiveness is conferred in ways that are distinctly context-dependent. That is, the grounding properties that confer the social property 'subversiveness' vary across different historical, geographical, and social contexts. For instance, in a context like China, works created in urban

96 Ásta Kristjana Sveinsdóttir, "Essentiality Conferred," *Philosophical Studies* 140, no. 1 (2008): 135–48, https://doi.org/10.1007/s11098-008-9230-4; Ásta Kristjana Sveinsdóttir, "Siding with Euthyphro: Response-Dependence and Conferred Properties," *European Journal of Philosophy* 18, no. 1 (2010): 108–25, https://doi.org/10.1111/j.1468-0378.2008.00303.x; Ásta Kristjana Sveinsdóttir, "The Social Construction of Human Kinds," *Hypatia* 28, no. 4 (2013): 716–32, https://doi.org/10.1111/j.1527-2001.2012.01317.x.

97 Sveinsdóttir, "The Social Construction of Human Kinds."

98 Sveinsdóttir, "Essentiality Conferred," 139.

99 Sveinsdóttir, "The Social Construction of Human Kinds," 721.

100 Sveinsdóttir, 723. Emphasis added.

101 Sveinsdóttir, 723.

styles – including the most radical forms of graffiti – are seldom considered subversive. As I have argued elsewhere, this is a consequence – among other things – of particular contextual features.[102] First, thanks to their impressive sizes, Chinese metropolises present an abundance of free spaces. Thus, conflicts about the use of visible surfaces tend not to emerge.[103] Second, practices of wall writing have a long history in China, and are still popular and widely carried out. For these reasons, Chinese people, in general, ignore markings on the walls and do not perceive them as rebellious intrusions within urban landscapes.[104] This, in turn, shows that the conferral of subversiveness is the outcome of a judgement evaluating specific features and their significance within a specific context. What is subversive in one place need not be subversive in another.

As I have mentioned, it is my view that 'subversiveness' is not only a social property, but also a holistic one. There are various ways to understand the exact nature of holistic properties. In general, the notion of holism refers to particular relationships between parts and wholes, which in these cases are interconnected in special ways. For the purpose of our present discussion, I characterize holistic properties in a sense that draws from Jerry Fodor's and Ernest Lepore's discussion of holism about meaning and content.[105] They write: "Holistic properties are such that, if anything has them, then lots of other things must have them too."[106]

In the context of this discussion of street art, when I say that 'being subversive' (or 'subversiveness') is a holistic property, what I intend is that if any street artwork is subversive, then lots of other particulars connected to the practice of street art must be subversive too. Such particulars include of course other street artworks, but – as I have already mentioned – also many other aspects and features belonging to street art as a whole, that is, the various sociological, cultural, technical, and political elements that characterize the practice. For instance, the ways in which graffiti writers live their lives, which Ricardo

---

102 Baldini, "Street Art: A Reply to Riggle."

103 Ally Thibault, "Beijing's Thriving Graffiti Culture May Surprise You," *Public Radio International*, accessed May 25, 2015, http://www.pri.org/stories/2014-04-21/beijings-thriving-graffiti-culture-may-surprise-you.

104 Lu Pan, "Writing at the End of History: Reflections on Two Cases of Graffiti in Hong Kong," *Public Art Dialogue* 4, no. 1 (2014): 147–66, https://doi.org/10.1080/21502552.2014.878487; Minna Valjakka, "Graffiti in China – Chinese Graffiti?," *The Copenhagen Journal of Asian Studies* 29, no. 1 (2011): 61–91.

105 Jerry A. Fodor and Ernest LePore, *Holism: A Shopper's Guide* (Oxford, UK and Cambridge, MA: Blackwell, 1992). Here, I am not interested in meaning holism. Therefore, I am ignoring Fodor's and Lepore's discussion about that view and its potential complications.

106 Fodor and LePore, 2.

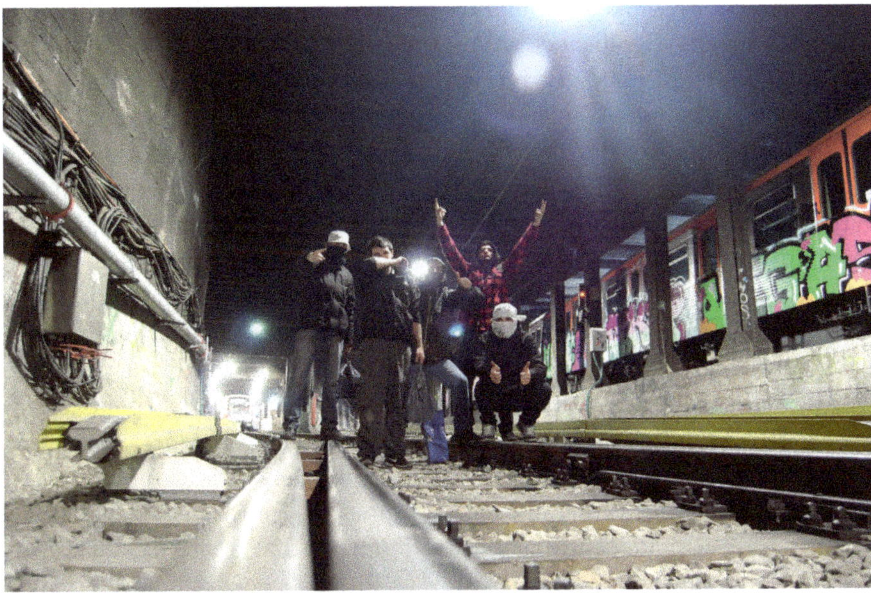

FIGURE 3 Italian, Australian, and Greek writers meet in the tunnels of Athens's subway
PHOTOGRAPH COURTESY OF FRA32

Campos perspicuously characterizes as "super hero" lives, subvert acceptable ways of living in modern societies.[107] In other words, just like street artworks, writers' lives are also subversive (fig. 3). Within their connection(s), all of these particulars taken as a whole acquire subversiveness as a holistic property.

The characterization of subversiveness as a social holistic property just offered provides us with enough conceptual resources to explain the relationship between street art and illegality. 'Being illegal' functions as one of those grounding properties guiding the conferral of the social holistic properties 'being subversive.' Of course, the conferral is not determined by the illegality of a work per se. Nonetheless, it is a feature that, in many contexts, is significantly connected with evaluating a street artwork as subversive. 'Being illegal' is therefore a salient property of street art. The holistic nature of 'being subversive' also suggests that, if 'being illegal' is a likely grounding property for subversiveness, then many street artworks will arguably be illegal. Here, illegality appears to be a recurrent property of street artworks.[108]

---

107 Ricardo Campos, "Graffiti Writer as Superhero," *European Journal of Cultural Studies* 16, no. 2 (2013): 155–70, https://doi.org/10.1177/1367549412467177.

108 By identifying illegality as a likely and not a necessary grounding property, my goal is to make room for the possibility of legal works that are nonetheless subversive. There might

Understood as a likely grounding property of subversiveness, illegality acquires a specific significance within the context of street art. According to my view, the significance of street artists' engagement with illegal activities cannot be simply understood in terms of a form of joy – a carnivalesque *jouissance* – depending on a feeling accompanying the transgression of the law.[109] In spite of street artists' conscious and explicit intentions, their actions holistically connect with the whole practice of street art, thus acquiring – as a consequence of such relationships – a specific type of political significance.

The aesthetic-political dimension of street art also allows us to understand its distinction from artistic phenomena such as forgery or latrinalia that also tend to challenge legal norms. Forgeries (tend to) defy the law, but it is difficult to see how – at least at a general level – these works could carry a political significance. In a similar sense, the isolated gesture of an exuberant lover writing "Baby I love you" on a bathroom door seems to have no political significance. It does not possess political significance insofar as this gesture – like that of the forger – does not significantly connect to a practice that is socially and holistically judged as subversive.

In concluding this chapter, what I have suggested could be generally summarized as follows: illegality is a salient and recurrent property of street art. Creating illegal street artworks is a strategy – a tactic or tool – whereby street artists can imbue their works with the subversiveness that, holistically, the practice of street art socially carries within itself. In other words, through the response elicited in passersby and viewers, the violation of the law is sometimes constitutive of a street artwork's meaning. This is turn shapes how the public reacts to the practice of street art considered as a whole, that is, globally. In the following chapter, I draw on this insight in order to answer a

---

be cases where artists create images that are apparently innocent, but are instead imbued with a 'hidden' meaning that is known to an underground community and potentially threatens an authority. Plausible examples of this kind in street art include works from the Frankfurt based project "Under Art Construction." See Andrea Baldini, "An Urban Carnival on the City Walls: The Visual Representation of Financial Power in European Street Art," *Journal of Visual Culture* 14, no. 2 (2015): 246–52, https://doi.org/10.1177/1470412915592883; Brighenti, "Graffiti, Street Art and the Divergent Synthesis of Place Valorisation in Contemporary Urbanism," 164–65. When considering other art kinds, calypso music in Haiti or some reggae songs in Jamaica can offer instructive examples, too.

109 In his interview with Mubi Brighenti, Italian graffiti writer Paolins talks about "infottamento," which could be understood as a form of *jouissance*. See Brighenti, "At the Wall," 320. I discuss street art as a carnivalesque practice in Baldini, "An Urban Carnival on the City Walls"; Baldini, "Quand les murs de béton muets se transforment en un carnaval de couleur."

question that has traditionally been accompanying discussions of street art: Is it art or vandalism?

## Part 2. (Not) Above the Law: Art or Vandalism?

### 1 *Introduction*

Since the emergence of (modern) graffiti on the walls of North American cities in the 1960s, the question of whether examples of street art are products of an art practice or mere criminal activities of a juvenile variety has certainly dominated everyday discourse on spontaneous urban art.[110] Scholarly debates on street art have also paid attention to what I call the *vandalism question*, that is, "Is it art or vandalism?"[111] But what are the assumptions that the vandalism question carries within itself? What exactly are we asking when considering whether street art is art or vandalism? Can't something be both artistically valuable and not legally sanctioned?

In this chapter, by considering these meta- or second-order questions, I suggest two ways in which one can plausibly construe the vandalism question. However, I will also show that both of the interpretations I will put forward have severe limitations. The dualism that the vandalism question presupposes cannot offer a suitable framework for understanding street art and its relationship with the law. I then argue that not only can street art be both art *and* vandalism, but also that street art is art because of its vandalistic nature. In saying that street art is art because of it is vandalism, I mean that vandalism

---

110 In historically connecting street art to the emergence of graffiti, I am favoring a particular narrative. This choice is, of course, far from necessary or uniquely valid. There are other possible stories of street art, which connect this art kind to other urban forms of artistic expression that emerged around the 1960s or even before. As I discuss in the Introduction, my choice is motivated by a particular philosophical conception of street art's identity. I see street art as a subversive art kind opposing mainstream art. As Joe Austin suggests, placing street art and its original genre, graffiti, in continuity with other art forms may very well jeopardize our possibility to understand the specificity of this art kind. See Austin, "More to See than a Canvas in a White Cube." For a sample of alternative historical narratives of street art, see "The History of Street Art," *Widewalls*, accessed September 20, 2018, https://www.widewalls.ch/the-history-of-street-art; "Thinking About the Origins of Street Art, Part 1," *Hyperallergic*, December 16, 2010, https://hyperallergic.com/14166/origins-of-street-art/.

111 See, among others, Marisa A. Gomez, "The Writing on Our Walls: Finding Solutions through Distinguishing Graffiti Art from Graffiti Vandalism," *University of Michigan Journal of Law Reform* 26 (1993): 633–708; McAuliffe and Iveson, "Art and Crime (and Other Things Besides ...)."

is a technique that street artists often use to realize street art's essential value, that is, its subversiveness.

Section 2 introduces some basic notions that are key to analyzing the logic of the vandalism question. In Section 3, I critically discuss the first possible interpretation of the vandalism question which draws on the right of speech. I also show its limitations. Section 4 examines an alternative interpretation of the vandalism question, which looks at the added aesthetic value that street art brings to the city landscape. I will dismiss this interpretation as also being unreasonable. Section 5 discusses my alternative view of the relationship between art and vandalism, wherein I suggest that vandalism is an artistic technique or tool central to the practice of street art.

## 2 *Discrete Concepts, Exclusive Disjunctions, and the Logic of the Vandalism Question*

Questions of the form "Is *x* an *a* or a *b*?" generally imply the truth of an exclusive disjunction between *a* or *b*. Exclusive disjunctions are of a variety such that, when true, it cannot be the case that both disjuncts have the same truth-value. That is, it cannot be the case that they are both true or both false. Let us take a moment to explain this claim step-by-step.

In the question "Is *x* an *a* or a *b*?" *a* and *b* identifies two discrete concepts. Discrete concepts are concepts that divide the totality of particulars into two subsets: one subset is the subset of those particulars to which the concept applies, the other subset picks out all those particulars to which the concept does not apply. For example, 'pear' is a discrete concept insofar as it divides the particulars in the world into two subsets: the subset of those particulars that are pears and the one of particulars that are not pears.

When we ask a question like "Is *x* an *a* or a *b*?" in a meaningful way, the discrete concepts expressed in the disjuncts should refer to some particulars in the world and should *not* have common elements. In other words, for the exclusive disjunction "*a* or *b*" to be true, there need to be some things that are *a* or *b*, and the intersection between *a* and *b* must be empty. In an ordinary context of usage, the question "Is this fruit an apple or a pear?" makes sense when 'apple' and 'pear' are two discrete concepts, whose respective extensions contain some elements, and whose intersection is an empty set. In other words, that question makes sense if there are things like pears and apples but there is no single particular that is both an apple and a pear.[112]

112 As far as I know, there are no known hybrids of pears and apples. In this sense, the intersection of pears and apples seems to be empty. Perhaps genetic manipulation technology will soon change that.

By the same token, in order to talk in a reasonable way about this issue, the vandalism question necessarily presupposes the truth of an exclusive disjunction between the concepts of art and vandalism. Therefore, when asking whether something is art or vandalism, one is making the following theoretical assumptions: art and vandalism are (i) two discrete concepts referring to some particulars in the world; and, (ii) their intersection is an empty set. In the remainder of this section, I consider these two assumptions in turn.

Assumption (i) seems rather reasonable. Let us begin by considering whether the concept of art is a discrete concept. Surely there are things like artworks. Though the demarcation of the concept of art is highly contested, in principle we tend to agree that there are things in the world that are art and things that are not art.[113] Of course, the boundaries of art's demarcation may very well be porous and, as Arthur Danto famously argued, even commonplace objects like boxes of Brillo pads and urinals can become art.[114] However, once artistically "transfigured," as Danto would say, a particular cannot be *both* an art object and a non-art object. The concept of art is not ontologically vague. Andy Warhol's *Brillo Box* and Marcel Duchamp's *Fountain*, for instance, are art, and *not* non-art – even though they are also commonplace objects.

With the concept of 'vandalism', things are even more clear-cut. Here, I explicitly understand the concept of vandalism in terms of the law, that is, as a notion identifying a particular subset of illegal actions, with all the formal implications that I have discussed in Chapter 1. Vandalism generally refers to acts of "[d]efacing or damaging property."[115] In most legal systems, vandalistic activities constitute an offence of criminal damage, which, for example, in UK legislation, the Criminal Damage Act 1971 defines as the "offence of intentionally or recklessly destroying or damaging any property belonging to another without a lawful excuse."[116]

Of course the complexity of real life scenarios may very well create difficulties in legal judgments about the status of particular actions. However, at least

113 For instructive surveys and critical discussion of the issue of demarcation in art, see Tiziana Andina, *The Philosophy of Art: The Question of Definition: From Hegel to Post-Dantian Theories* (London: Bloomsbury Academic, 2013); Tiziana Andina, *What Is Art?: The Question of Definition Reloaded* (Leiden: Brill, 2017).

114 Arthur C. Danto, "The Artworld," *The Journal of Philosophy* 61 (1964): 571–84; Arthur C. Danto, *The Transfiguration of the Commonplace: A Philosophy of Art* (Cambridge, MA: Harvard University Press, 1981).

115 Elizabeth Martin and Jonathan Law, "Vandalism," *A Dictionary of Law* (Oxford: Oxford University Press, 2015).

116 Elizabeth Martin and Jonathan Law, "Criminal Damage," *A Dictionary of Law* (Oxford: Oxford University Press, 2015).

in principle, the formality of the law and its procedures allows us to distinguish between vandalism and non-vandalism in a rather straightforward way. Moreover, as a consequence of its formality, the vagueness of the concept of vandalism is – similarly to the case of art – not ontological: however one understands such a legal predicate, any particular action will either be vandalistic or it won't be. For this reason, vandalism is certainly a discrete concept that refers to particulars in the world.

In claiming that the intersection between the concept of 'art' and the concept of 'vandalism' is empty, assumption (ii) implies, among other things, the following: there is no given particular *p* (either an object, an event, an action, or anything else) that is at the same time both an example of art and an instance of vandalism. In other words, on the one hand, an artwork cannot be vandalistic. On the other hand, vandalism is not art. If the particular *p* has artistic status (or perhaps value) and falls within the extension of 'art', then, according to (ii), *p* cannot also be an example of 'vandalism'.

Assumption (ii) appears much less intuitive than assumption (i). In light of the conceptual analysis developed above, it is in effect not immediately clear why a given particular *p* cannot be both art and vandalism. There seems to be no self-evident relationship of exclusive opposition between the concept of 'art' and the concept of 'vandalism'. Apparently, these two concepts do not seem to point in the direction of some ontological gap that could warrant an assumption about their disjunction.

Yet, by considering the popularity of the discussion both in everyday and scholarly discourse, it seems important to construe the vandalism question in the most charitable way so that it can actually make sense. In order to fully unpack, clarify, and address this discussion about street art and its relationship with the law, and to offer a comprehensive reply to the vandalism question, it is important to signal what discussants may be intending to say when considering this issue. That is, it is useful to understand how the exclusive disjunction "art or vandalism" can be true. In the following section, I offer a first plausible construal of the vandalism question, which appeals to the right to speak freely.

## 3 *Art, Freedom of Speech, and Vandalism*

One plausible way to construe the vandalism question so that the exclusive disjunction that it implies turns out to be true, in summary, is the following one. It starts by assuming that art is a form of free speech, and that an artwork is akin or analogous to an artist's linguistic utterances. Just as forms of free speech are (and should be) protected by laws such as the First Amendment to the United States Constitution, artworks should also be similarly protected.

The destruction or criminalization of 'utterances' of artistic creativity as acts of vandalism, then, amounts to censorship. In order to protect our freedom of speech, we should not outlaw art even in problematic instances where its content, forms, or placement raise legal concerns. In this case, the intersection of art and vandalism is (would be) empty, insofar as artworks cannot belong, under any circumstances, to the category of criminal activities. Call this proposal the *argument from freedom of speech.*

This view finds one of its most explicit and vocal advocates in internationally acclaimed artist Richard Serra. Serra first presented this view in 1989, at the pinnacle of the *Tilted Arc* controversy.[117] I expect that many readers are already familiar with the story of *Tilted Arc.*[118] Here is a quick recapitulation. The Art-in-Architecture Program of the General Services Administration (GSA) awarded a commission to Serra in 1979 to create a public artwork in one of the squares of New York City: Federal Plaza. The artist's project was to realize a monumental site-specific installation that could shape and re-shape the nature of the plaza: the *Tilted Arc.* Probably the most discussed example of 20th century public art, the *Arc* was a slightly curved wall in Cor-Ten steel. It was 120 ft long, 12 ft high, and 2.5 in thick.

Serra envisioned his monumental *Tilted Arc* as occupying the middle of Federal Plaza, interrupting the most natural way for passers-by to cut across the square. Miwon Kwon correctly suggests that Serra's choices of design and placement were intended to serve the following purpose: "to interrogate rather than accommodate the given architecture, [and to disrupt] the spatial conditions of the art work's site at Federal Plaza in New York City".[119]

Serra's words goes in the direction of Kwon's reading of the situation when he writes:

---

117 Richard Serra, "Tilted Arc Destroyed," *Art in America* 77 (1989): 34–47; Richard Serra, "Art and Censorship," *Nova Law Review* 14, no. 2 (1990): 323–32; Richard Serra, "Tilted Arc Destroyed," *Nova Law Review* 14, no. 2 (1990): 385–406; Richard Serra, "Art and Censorship," *Critical Inquiry* 17, no. 3 (1991): 574–81. See also Susan Duke Biederman, ed., "Symposium on Law and the Visual Arts," *Nova Law Review* 14, no. 2 (1990): 305–582.

118 Arthur C. Danto, "Tilted Arc and Public Art," in *The State of the Art* (New York, NY: Prentice-Hall Press, 1987); Gregg M. Horowitz, "Public Art/Public Space: The Spectacle of the Tilted Arc Controversy," *The Journal of Aesthetics and Art Criticism* 54, no. 1 (1996): 8–14; Harriet F. Senie, "Richard Serra's 'Tilted Arc': Art and Non-Art Issues," *Art Journal* 48, no. 4 (1989): 298–392; Harriet F. Senie, *The Tilted Arc Controversy: Dangerous Precedent?* (Ann Arbor, MI: University of Minnesota Press, 2002).

119 Miwon Kwon, *One Place After Another: Site-Specific Art and Locational Identity* (Cambridge, MA: MIT Press, 2004), 5.

> As I [Serra] pointed out, *Tilted Arc* was conceived from the start as a site-specific sculpture [...]. Site-specific works deal with the environmental components of given places. The scale, size, and location of site-specific works are determined by the topography of the site, whether it be urban or landscape or architectural enclosure. The works become part of the site and restructure both conceptually and perceptually the organization of the site.[120]

The aggressive design and placement of Serra's *Arc* generated adverse reactions in part of its public. These reactions picked up momentum just a few years after the installation of the piece, which appeared in the middle of Federal Plaza in 1981. The critical wave resulted in five years of public hearings, lawsuits, and controversies, which became a central element of the brief history of the public reception of *Tilted Arc*. The installation was dismantled and removed from Federal Plaza on March 15 1989, roughly ten years after Serra received the commission from the GSA for this piece.

While opposing the removal of his installation and later on criticizing the decision of relocating – and, in the artist's view, destroying – the piece, Serra proposed an argument that appeals to the First Amendment and the freedom of speech. He clearly implies that *Tilted Arc*, and arguably art in general, is an expression of speech. This view echoes some important strands in philosophy of art that construe artworks' meaning and interpretation in terms of a conversational model. According to this model, when appreciating and interpreting artworks, we enter a relationship with artists that is "roughly analogous" to having a conversation with them.[121] In these sense, artworks are akin to the utterances of artists.

As expressions of an artist's speech, artworks share the same rights that we acknowledge to the free expression of opinions, and therefore authorities should protect them in a similar way. As Serra's attorneys claimed in the appeal filed against the decision of removing *Tilted Arc*, "once a medium of expression – be it writing, film, theater, painting or sculpture – is publicly installed or displayed, first amendment rights attach which prohibit the government from removing the expression on the basis of its content."[122] The right to speak freely should protect works of art, too.

120 Serra, "Tilted Arc Destroyed," 1990, 397.

121 Noël Carroll, "Art, Intention, and Conversation," in *Intention and Interpretation*, ed. Gary Iseminger (Philadelphia, PA: Temple University Press, 1992), 117.

122 From *Serra v. General Services Administration* as cited in Serra, "Tilted Arc Destroyed," 1990, 400.

In this sense, the destruction of an artwork is, for Serra, tantamount to an attempt "to censor and destroy speech".[123] It is an act that violates – in his own words – the "right to free speech."[124] As a violation of this fundamental right, authorities' destroying artworks, Serra suggests, has at least two significant implications, which are relevant to our discussion. The first is that, by destroying artworks possessing properties of design and location similar to those of *Tilted Arc*, but not others that differs in those respects, authorities reclaim "the right to judge the content of art" while applying "bogus standards of decency and civility."[125]

The second significant implication of authorities destroying artworks is as follows. As the courts affirmed, "Serra sold his 'speech' to the Government. [...] As such, his 'speech' became "property in 1981, when he received full payment for his work. [...] An owner's '[p]roperty rights in a physical thing [allow him] to possess, use and dispose of it.'"[126] The motivation legally warranting the decision of removing *Titled Arc*, Serra claims, "affirms the government's commitment to private property over the interests of art or free expression."[127] This appears morally unjust to Serra: property rights should not supersede freedom of speech.

With these two implications in mind, it is easy to understand how Serra's argument could be reasonably extended to street art. By following Serra's reasoning, one could say that street art deserves to be treated as other forms of art. In effect, discriminating against street art on the basis of its style(s) and placement would amount to that same disputable application of "bogus standards of decency and civility" that Serra denounces in his article.[128] It should not matter how street art looks or how it occupies public space: as expressions of free speech, street artworks should not be criminalized.

Moreover – perhaps even more importantly – the criminalization and destruction of street artworks as forms of vandalism, one could also add, show authorities' commitment to private property over freedom of expression. However, this hierarchy appears to be morally flawed, if not backwards. Furthermore, one might add, if we take free speech as a cornerstone of our societies, such freedom should be an overriding reason even in the face of property owners' rights.

123 Serra, "Art and Censorship," 578.

124 Serra, 578.

125 Serra, 579, 581.

126 "Brief Filed by the Defendants, United States Court of Appeals for the Second Circuit, January 26, 1988 (edited)" in Serra, 575.

127 Serra, 575.

128 Serra, 581.

If one accepts the application of Serra's argument to cases of street art, then it seems that we have found a way to construe the vandalism question in a reasonable way. If freedom of speech should function as an overriding reason to accept controversial cases of street art (primarily, street artworks that have been realized in violation of laws regulating the uses of public and private spaces), then we have found a scenario where the exclusive disjunction "(street) art or vandalism" would actually be true.[129]

The logic of this argument from freedom of speech seems to resonate with some recent legal decisions dealing with copyright issues in the context of street art.[130] (This will be the focus of Chapter 3.) However, because it is too radical, I believe that this view is significantly flawed. As such, it cannot offer a suitable framework for understanding the relationship between street art and vandalism, and we need to discard it. Let me offer two reasons as evidence for my dismissal of this interpretation of the vandalism question.

First, one need not be a philistine to find it implausible to say that no public or community standards of civility should be at play in evaluating certain examples of artistic expression. Postmodernist and poststructuralist thinkers have long argued that value systems are historically contingent.[131] Today, very few would find the idea that dominant conceptions of decorum and appropriate behavior are constructed and contested to be surprising. However, even in the profoundly heterogeneous and pluralistic societies we often find in today's world, it is relatively easy to come up with counterexamples to a universal acceptance of art. This in turn seems to strike a fatal blow against the radical view of freedom of speech and (artistic) expression.

Imagine an artwork that presents as its content scenes depicting pornographic images involving children. I struggle to even consider the option that

129 The argument from freedom of speech may very well give the impression that I am endorsing the idea that street art is not distinct art kind, but it is better understood in continuity with traditional art forms. I hasten to add that I do not believe this to be the case. General theories or definition of art seem doomed to fail. By following Dom Lopes's buck-passing theory, it is my view that to be a work of art is to be a work in a particular art kind. See Lopes, *Beyond Art*, 11–15.

130 See, for instance, Alan Feuer, "Graffiti Artists Awarded $6.7 Million for Destroyed 5Pointz Murals," *The New York Times*, February 13, 2018, sec. New York, https://www.nytimes.com/2018/02/12/nyregion/5pointz-graffiti-judgment.html; Alan Feuer, "Brooklyn Lawsuit Asks If Illegal Graffiti Is Protected by Copyright Law," *The New York Times*, March 15, 2018, sec. New York, https://www.nytimes.com/2018/03/15/nyregion/brooklyn-graffiti-hm-lawsuit.html.

131 See, for instance, Michel Foucault, *Discipline and Punish: The Birth of the Prison* (New York: Vintage Books, 1995).

those who would protest against an artwork of this kind could be legitimately labelled as authoritarian individuals, whose dissenting amounts to a violation of a fundamental right such as the freedom of speech. For instance, I do not find something illiberal in the recent wave of protest against the controversial painting *Thérèse Dreaming*, created in 1938 by Polish-French artist Balthus.[132] As is well known, the painting represents a young girl, Thérèse Blanchard, who was a neighbor of the artist at the time. Some formal and symbolic elements of the painting such as the girl's pose and the cat licking milk warrant, according to some, a sexualized interpretation of the painting. In November 2017, circa 9000 individuals signed a petition asking for the removal of the painting from the walls of the Met, where the painting is currently exhibited. I remain neutral about this controversy. It is not my goal here to address the details of this issue and to offer an opinion. However, I do not find these concerns necessary signs of obtuseness.

As the philosopher Anthony O'Hear suggests, struggles and controversies of public art should be taken seriously, for they are often expressions of significant differences, and not necessarily symptoms of ignorance. In discussing famous cases of controversial publicly sponsored art, including Andres Serrano's *Piss Christ* and Robert Mapplethorpe's photographs, he writes the following:

> The public funding of the arts raises questions about public taste and decency which ought to be addressed more directly than they often are and that people involved in the arts should be far more honest and open about what they are about if they choose to dwell on what is negative and disgusting in human life. I mean that while an artist might choose to depict scenes of, let us say, atrocities and the like as therapy for himself, a question is raised as to the attitude normal people should take to such work.[133]

Second, it seems once again too radical to claim that property owners' rights should never have primacy over the interests of art and freedom of expression. To be clear, I am generally critical of tendencies of commodification of public space in modern liberal cities. The reduction of public space to an enabler of commercial interactions (including advertising) is a transformation that

132 "The Met Says 'Suggestive' Balthus Painting Will Stay After Petition for Its Removal Is Signed by Thousands," *artnet News*, December 5, 2017, https://news.artnet.com/art-world/met-museum-responds-to-petition-calling-for-removal-of-balthus-painting-1169105.

133 Anthony O'Hear, "Art and Censorship," *Philosophy* 66, no. 258 (1991): 516.

is impoverishing our everyday lives and our possibilities of self-expression.[134] However, even from my critical standpoint, I agree with Enrico Bonadio when he argues that there is a tension between the rights of an artist and the rights of an owner that cannot be resolved in the abstract, but only in a case-by-case fashion.[135]

While discussing issues of destruction of street artworks, Bonadio writes: "there is a strong tension between artists and owners of the surfaces where artworks are placed. [However] there is little doubt that in certain circumstances artists should accept the fact that placing their works on others' properties may carry the risk of losing control over the tangible medium".[136] This balanced approach, which contemplates the possibility of ad hoc decisions, seems to me more reasonable that Serra's radical view.

At this point, one could wonder whether it is possible to advance a more moderate version of the argument from freedom of speech according to which artistic expression should be protected from censorship, provided that it does not trespass certain standards. This argument is certainly plausible (even convincing), but it is useless in this context. It is highly unlikely that something as controversial as violating property laws could pass as acceptable in most countries. Arguably, criminal damage would be upheld as one of the standards that artistic expression as free speech should not trespass. Even if a moderate version of the argument from freedom of speech could work for some art kinds, it could do little when considering street art.

In this section, I have showed the limitations of the argument from freedom of speech. I suggested that, though a fundamental human right, the right to speak freely cannot always provide sufficient legal grounds for accepting an act of artistic expression. Sometimes, other concerns or considerations may very well warrant considering an artwork as a form of vandalism and criminal activity, with all the consequences that this implies. In the following section, I offer another possible way to understand that question, which depends on considerations of value.

---

134 Baldini, "Street Art: A Reply to Riggle"; Baldini, "Quand les murs de béton muets se transforment en un carnaval de couleur"; Baldini, "An Urban Carnival on the City Walls."

135 Enrico Bonadio, "Copyright Protection of Street Art and Graffiti under UK Law," SSRN Scholarly Paper (Rochester, NY: Social Science Research Network, 2017), https://papers.ssrn.com/abstract=2946360.

136 Bonadio, 19–20.

## 4 *Aesthetic Value, Urban Beauty, and the Law*

In early 2016, Judge Gabriella Castore found Alice Pasquini, whose street name is AliCè, guilty of criminal defacement of property.[137] Some works that AliCè realized without authorization or consent a few years earlier on the walls of Bologna, a city in Northern Italy, were the object of the ruling. In replying to Judge Castore's decision during an interview with journalist Michele Smargiassi from the Italian newspaper *La Repubblica*, AliCè offers some insights that one can use as a foundation for a possible interpretation of the vandalism question.[138] Let me first develop her insights explicitly into an argument. Then, I will show the limitations of such a view.

By commenting the result of her trial, AliCè aired her discontent and claimed:

> I [AliCè] am disappointed: Saatchi Gallery in London had just exhibited some of my works. One can find my works at auctions or museums in more than 50 countries around the world. I am always the same person, when I work on commission or when I paint in the street. So, people should take a position: am I an artist or a vandal?

Here, she tackles the vandalism question and connects it to the issue of aesthetic value.

One could sum up the core thesis that AliCè presents in this interview as follows: Some works of street art beautify the sites where they are installed and, therefore, they add aesthetic value to those places. Of course, locations must present specific features insofar as they should lack – prior to intervention – aesthetic, artistic, or historic value: "I would never paint on a clean wall, even less on a monument. [I] choose small spaces on already degraded walls."[139] In these cases, the added aesthetic value that the installation of a street artwork brings to its site functions as an overriding principle in deliberations of vandalism and criminal damage. Call this argument the *argument from beauty*.

---

137 One can find a useful selection of newspaper articles on this episode in the following blogpost "Caso di Alice Pasquini, street artist conosciuta come AliCè," accessed June 10, 2018, http://www.associazioneantigraffiti.it/2016/02/21/caso-di-alice-pasquini-street-artist-conosciuta-come-alice/.

138 "Caso di Alice Pasquini, street artist conosciuta come AliCè."

139 "Caso di Alice Pasquini, street artist conosciuta come AliCè."

If the argument from freedom of speech appealed to a basic moral right to make sense of the exclusive disjunction between art and vandalism, the argument from beauty brings to the table aesthetic considerations. If for the first interpretation of the vandalism question that I have here examined it is morally wrong to consider expressions of artistic freedom as criminal acts, in this case beauty provides us with an overriding reason for dismissing charges of criminal damages. In other words, when a particular example *p* of street art increases the aesthetic value of a portion of the city, that is, when *p* makes the urban landscape more beautiful, then *p* should never be considered as an instance of vandalism or criminal activity.

Though the argument from beauty points towards an interesting direction, I still believe that it suffers from fatal flaws. I am sympathetic to the idea that the law should pay more attention to matters of beauty. With that said, I hasten to add, aesthetic value should not function – as we shall see in the remainder of this section and in the following one – as an overriding reason in legal deliberations, including those about acceptable uses of private and public properties. That is, even the argument from beauty does not offer a plausible interpretative framework wherein the vandalism question makes sense. I can offer at list two reasons as evidence for my claim.

The first criticism against the argument from beauty points out the contested nature of aesthetic evaluations. This point echoes the motivation that Judge Castore offered as a justification for her ruling.[140] When refusing to accept AliCè's lawyer Stefania Martelli and public prosecutors' arguments for acquittal, Judge Castore claimed the following:

> the existence of the crime cannot have as parameter [...] the possible artistic nature of the artwork that one is creating. [For] evaluations of a painting's artistic value [are] a function of taste and social feelings or individual variables, often influenced by fashionable trends. [Though AliCè] is considered a talented artist among those who appreciate street art and similar artistic genres, those who value other artistic forms may very well disagree with that judgment.[141]

140 I have discussed this legal case in Baldini, "Beauty and the Behest."

141 Gianluca Rotondi, "Il giudice e la multa ad Alicè « La sua arte non basta »," *Corriere Di Bologna*, February 26, 2016, http://corrieredibologna.corriere.it/bologna/notizie/cronaca/2016/26-febbraio-2016/giudice-multa-ad-alice-la-sua-arte-non-basta-24099108117.shtml.

In the view of Judge Castore, aesthetic considerations do not offer solid ground for legal considerations.

One way to understand what Judge Castore is saying in her response to AliCè's lawyer and the public prosecutors draws on some insights that I have already discussed in Chapter 1 and in my previous work on what I have called the "structural differences" between aesthetic and legal judgment.[142] Arguably, one could say that two features significantly separate, on the one hand, evaluations in the domain of aesthetics, and, on the other, verdicts of the law: first, the absence of judges for aesthetics and, second, the impossibility of finding aesthetic laws. The conjunction of these two claims suggests extreme caution in accepting aesthetic considerations as having any legal import. Let me briefly consider both claims in turn.

When I say that there are no judges for aesthetics I am, of course, not claiming that there are no aesthetic experts or 'authorities.' However, as I have underlined in Chapter 1, I am pointing out that there is a significant distinction between aesthetic experts and legal judges: the latter, but not the former, are professionalized figures selected and appointed in terms of formalized curricula and procedures. Nothing comparable holds for aesthetic experts. It is true, in effect, as Dominic McIver Lopes notices, that "a fair sample draws aesthetic experts from many walks of life," not only professional art critics, art historians, curators, and philosophers of art deserve such a qualification.[143] In other words, comparing legal judges with aesthetic experts raises the following concern, that is, "the question that troubled (or should have troubled) Hume, namely 'By what marks do you recognize the authorities, the 'true [aesthetic] judges'?".[144]

Also, in the previous chapter, I have already introduced the key point explaining the absence of aesthetic laws in a proper sense. We don't have any criteria of application for non-innocuous aesthetic predicates to non-aesthetic features. On the contrary, as Mary Mothersill claims, where "there are formal definitions – [as in] parts of the law – there are criteria for the application of predicates."[145] With respect to this particular aspect, there are no aesthetic principles that function in the same way in which positive laws normally work. In a similar vein, Richard Wollheim also points out the absence of aesthetic laws in relationship with the kind of freedom characterizing artistic

142 Baldini, "Beauty and the Behest," 93–98. See also Chap. 1, 16–17.

143 Lopes, "Aesthetic Experts, Guides to Value," 326.

144 Mary Mothersill, "Aesthetics: The Need for a Theory," *Midwest Studies In Philosophy* 24, no. 1 (2000): 251, https://doi.org/10.1111/1475-4975.00033.

145 Mothersill, "Aesthetic Laws, Principles and Properties," 79. See also Mary Mothersill, *Beauty Restored* (Oxford, UK: Clarendon Press, 1984).

interpretation as well as, one might add, aesthetic evaluation: "over a great deal of art, the artist is characteristically operating at the intersection of more than one intention. It would therefore be quite alien to his purposes if there were rules in art that could be unambiguously correlated with a 'meaning'".[146] Aesthetic principles lack in the formality that makes positive laws useful within legal determinations.

Here is my second criticism against the argument from beauty. As AliCè emphasizes in her interview, the view that grounds this argument places more traditional forms of artistic expression and street art in a distinct continuity. In effect, it assumes aesthetic value as the essential value of street art. In this sense, we are dealing here with (the sketch of) a theory that denies any specificity to this form of spontaneous urban expression, and understands it as a practice whose goal is, primarily, to beautify urban environments.

The conceptual move of denying specificity to street art and its value raises the following concern: it collapses street art into more traditional forms of mainstream art. This consequence is unfortunate for at least the following reason. It makes the subversiveness of street art, and thus its recurrent and salient illegality, neutral with respect to the creation, appreciation, and interpretation of street artworks. To look at a street artwork would not be different in principle from looking at a painting in a museum or a decorative installation in a public square. This implication seems a *reductio ad absurdum* of the argument from beauty.

The kind of reduction that AliCè seems to suggest, in effect, leaves many questions unanswered and many doubts unresolved. Why would an artist engage in the first place in an activity that obviously violates current legislation regulating uses of private or public property? Why shouldn't artists spend their effort and time in creating art for galleries or projects of authorized public art? Why should they bother with dealing with the dangers necessarily associated with breaking the law? Monica Cuoghi, another prominent Italian street artist, raises exactly this concern when commenting on AliCè's words: "Artists should be aware that they are doing something illegal. It's part of the game, and in my opinion this is what makes it valuable" (fig. 4).[147]

It seems therefore that the argument from beauty also fails to offer us a viable candidate for construing the vandalism question. As a further consequence, it seems that this interpretation is also incapable of offering a suitable

146 Richard Wollheim, *Art and Its Objects* (Cambridge, UK: Cambridge University Press, 1980), 139.

147 "Caso di Alice Pasquini, street artist conosciuta come AliCè."

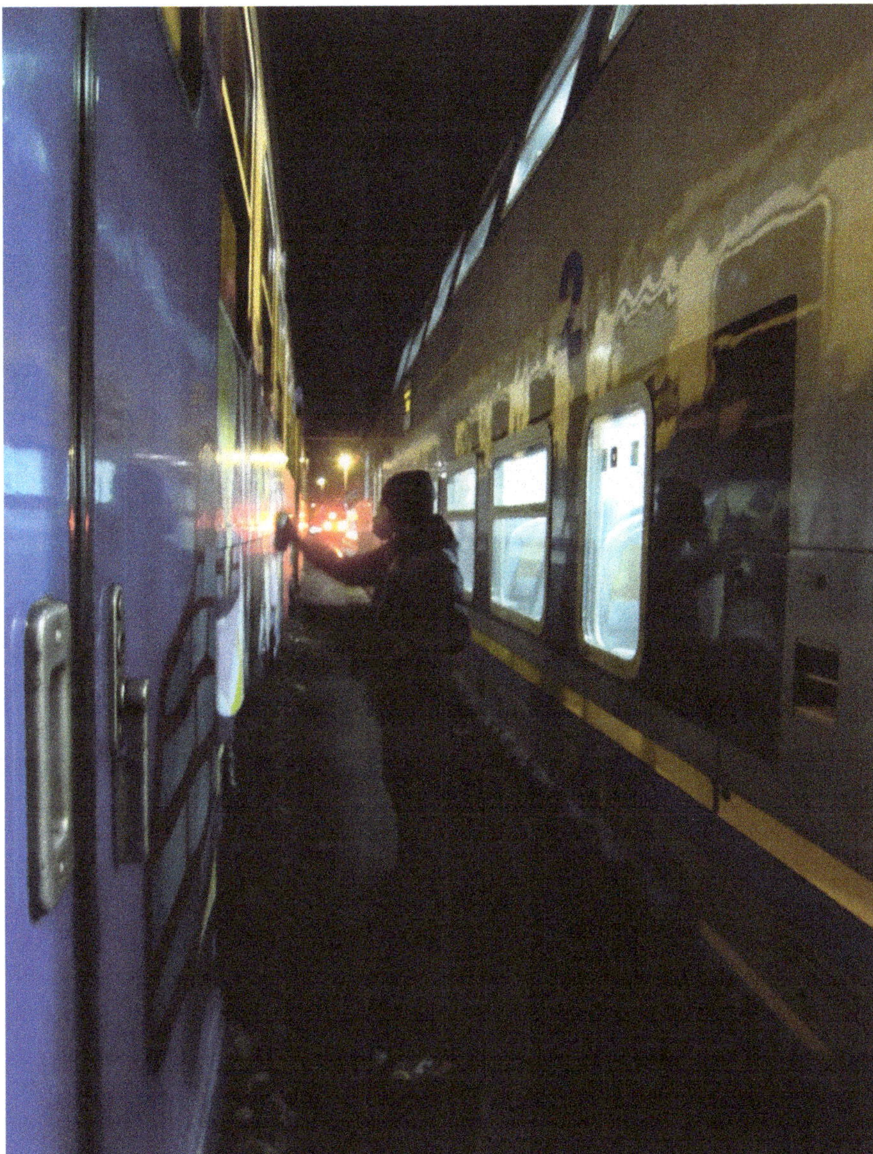

FIGURE 4 CHAOS painting in Italy
PHOTOGRAPH COURTESY OF FRA32

framework for further illuminating the relationship between street art and the law. So how should one proceed? In the following section, I offer my take on the vandalism question.

## 5 *It's Art Because It's Vandalism!*

The aim of this section is to propose a new approach to the vandalism question, and, *a fortiori*, a new approach to trying to understand the relationship between street art and the law. In brief, I propose the entire dismissal of the vandalism question and the rejection of the exclusive disjunction that it implies. I suggest that we should develop a framework that sees the artistic and vandalistic sides of street art as essentially related. Such a proposal is, I candidly admit, radical and requires a significant paradigm shift in the ways in which we conceptualize the link(s) connecting art, politics, and illegality.

My views here resonate sympathetically with Cameron McAuliffe's and Kurt Iveson's view. They see, as I do, that the exclusive disjunction between art and crime implied by the vandalism question is misleading. Moreover, they "want to suggest that [street art] might be both."[148] However, I also want to push my understanding even further. I do not want to just say that street art can be both art and vandalism, but that it is art, in some sense that I will specify in below, *partly* because of its vandalism. Let me clarify what I intend with this provocative claim.

In the previous sections, I have showed that, conceptually, the vandalism question is simply a non-starter in the attempt to illuminate at least some aspects of the relationship between street art and the law. In effect, as McAuliffe and Iveson correctly highlight, discussions that assume the truth of the exclusive disjunction between 'art' and 'vandalism' "rapidly reach an impasse."[149] Views that cannot accept the idea that a particular work of street art can be both art and vandalism seem to miss something crucial about the artistic phenomenon that they try to investigate.

On the one hand, when identifying illegal street artworks with mere examples of vandalism, one will have to ignore the artistic qualities of these particulars. McAuliffe and Iveson seem to be correct when they claim that "those who have advocated for the criminalisation of graffiti generally refuse to engage with the important question of what [street art] actually says or looks like [...] whether it is beautiful, hateful, insightful or dull."[150] Dissolving street art into mere vandalism reduces this urban phenomenon to an artistically uninteresting juvenile form of rebellion, comparable to vulgar forms of writings done on bathrooms walls and generally called latrinalia.[151] However, the attention

148 McAuliffe and Iveson, "Art and Crime (and Other Things Besides ...)," 130.

149 McAuliffe and Iveson, 130.

150 McAuliffe and Iveson, 131.

151 Latrinalia are erratic forms of expression lacking, it seems to me, a shared value that could make them an appreciative kind or art kind. I am not interested here in denying that latrinalia may be interesting in some ways. I am claiming that they are not valuable from an

that global audiences are paying to practices of street art seems a powerful rejection of this approach. Street art seems to be something more than mere vandalism.

On the other hand, while ignoring the vandalistic aspect of street art as significant, as I have showed in the last section, one is also bound to fail to notice the specificity of street art: by doing so, one is seriously running the risk of both collapsing this subversive art kind into traditional mainstream art and setting aside its subversiveness, which is importantly (though not exclusively) grounded in street art's illegality.[152] In this sense, as Michael Keith rightly points out, failing to see street art as a "technology of expression [that] challenges the very status of language, dialogue and discourse within the public sphere" whose goal is to "make multiculture visible" is a fatal shortcoming for an explanatory and interpretative framework.[153]

By building on Keith's claim, I suggest that we should understand street art as a "technology of resistance."[154] Michael Bernhard defines technology of resistance as the set of those methods and tactics that underground groups deploy to challenge authority. Underground groups are incapable of directly transforming laws or the organization of a political system: They do not possess such power. However, thanks to technologies of resistance, they can initiate

---

artistic point of view. For a discussion of latrinalia, see Adrian Birney, "Crack Puns: Text and Context in an Item of Latrinalia," *Western Folklore* 32, no. 2 (1973): 137–40, https://doi.org/10.2307/1498326; Alan Dundes, *Meaning of Folklore: The Analytical Essays of Alan Dundes* (Logan: Utah State University Press, 2007).

152 Traditional mainstream art includes artworks of all those art kinds such as painting, sculpture, installation art, etching, etc. that we usually find exhibited in museums and galleries, sold at auctions, taught in art schools, researched and critically discussed in scholarly works. Recently, it is possible to find works of some street artists like AliCè in galleries and museums. Here, I am not interested in airing the potential issues which arise from this phenomenon. For a discussion of the problem of street art's musealization, see Rivasi and Baldini, *Un(Authorized)//Commissioned*; Peter Bengtsen, "Carelessness or Curatorial Chutzpah? On Controversies Surrounding Street Art in the Museum," *Konsthistorisk Tidskrift/Journal of Art History* 84, no. 4 (2015): 220–33, https://doi.org/10.1080/00233609.2015.1095797. For a discussion of mainstream culture and art, see Hannerz, *Performing Punk*.

153 Michael Keith, *After the Cosmopolitan? Multicultural Cities and the Future of Racism* (London; New York: Routledge, 2005), 136. See also Austin, *Taking the Train*; Austin, "More to See than a Canvas in a White Cube"; Baldini, "Street Art: A Reply to Riggle"; Baldini, "Quand les murs de béton muets se transforment en un carnaval de couleur"; Iveson, *Publics and the City*.

154 Michael Bernhard, "The Polish Opposition and the Technology of Resistance," 3, http://www.clas.ufl.edu/users/bernhard/content/Solid3.pdf; Benjamin B. Fischer, "Solidarity, the CIA, and Western Technology," *International Journal of Intelligence and CounterIntelligence* 25, no. 3 (2012): 428, https://doi.org/10.1080/08850607.2012.652523.

change from the ground up, which can eventually lead to a deeper political transformation. Street art is a technology of resistance in this sense: it provides some underground groups with methods and tactics to challenge authority and, in particular, what I have called the *corporate regime of visibility*.[155]

It is this significant aspect of street art as a technology of resistance that, as I have anticipated, invites us to say more about the relationship between art and vandalism in the context of street art than simply admitting their conjunction. There is an essential relationship between art and vandalism. Only by clarifying such a link can one gain clarity about the connection between street art and the law, a connection that has puzzled theorists, authorities, and lay people alike since the emergence of modern graffiti.

When I say that street art is art partly because of its vandalism, I hasten to add, I am *not* suggesting that there is a counterfactual causal connection between the artistic nature of street art and its vandalistic quality. To be even more explicit, I should also specify that being vandalistic is neither a necessary nor a sufficient condition for a street artwork to be art. I have something different in mind that does not imply or indicate such a strong logical and metaphysical link between art and vandalism. A strict causal connection would be too demanding to be plausible as well as theoretically at odds with – if not contradictory to – my discussion in Chapter 1.

The claim that street art is art because of its vandalism should be interpreted as follows: Street artists characteristically use vandalism as an artistic resource that significantly informs processes of creation, appreciation, evaluation, and interpretation within the practice of street art intended as a whole. This in turn also captures a significant fact about the history of street art. Part of its artistic meaning and significance depends on the use of vandalism as an artistic device. In particular, vandalism is a crucial technique by means of which street artworks are imbued with the variety of subversiveness that is an essential feature of this urban art kind which I have discussed in Chapter 1.[156]

It is my view, then, that street art is an aesthetic-political practice, which characteristically (or paradigmatically) uses vandalism as a tactic to express (and enact) its subversive nature and goals. Street art is an aesthetic practice insofar as it creates meaning through the materiality of its forms and their perception in the viewers' experiences. In other words, it is by engaging

155 See Introduction. This point also echoes Bacharach's discussion of street art and activism. See Bacharach, "Finding Your Voice in the Streets."

156 According to Lopes, techniques partly constitute the medium profile of works in an art kind. From such a perspective, vandalism is an aspect of street art's medium profile. See Lopes, *Beyond Art*, 139–40.

perceptually with the shapes, colors, designs, lines, textures, etc. of a street artwork that we can appreciate its value(s), meaning(s), and significance. It is also political to the extent that – as a subversive practice and a technology of resistance – aspects of its value(s), meaning(s), and significance(s) possess a political undertone.[157] A full-fledged understanding of street art must acknowledge the *hybrid* (both aesthetic and political) nature of this art kind.

Austin has done a good job of highlighting the artistic import of street art.[158] He characterizes street art as "a new departure in the history of modern art, and this departure opens up new potentials for modernism".[159] The most relevant contributions that street art can offer are found in two areas: first, the Modern separation of art and life, and, second, the commodification of the artistic object. Street art challenges both these trends that dominate modern practices of art, and vandalism – as a source of subversiveness – is key for obtaining such achievements.

When thinking about the challenge of the Modern separation of art and life, Austin adds that street art resembles provocations of the *dada* movement in the 1920s and the development of *pop-art* of the 1950s and 1960s.[160] Similarly to street art, by respectively bringing common objects into galleries or appropriating the language(s) of urban communication, both *dada* and *pop-art* conceptually established a connection between everyday life and art. It is part of their historical significance as artistic movements. Street art, on its part, does that while lacking the irony or detachment typical of those two art movements. Furthermore, it literally intrudes on the city's daily spaces by reshaping their uses and how we perceive them.[161] This is possible also thanks to the use of vandalism, which enters in an immediate conflict with the legal order and its impact on dominant spatial politics.

157 Art can be political in many ways: subversive art is only one possibility among a wide range. Memorials and monuments are often examples of political art that is celebratory and not subversive. Propaganda art is political insofar as it promotes the values and ideas endorsed by a particular political party or government. For a discussion of political art, see Thijs Lijster et al., "Politics," in *Encyclopedia of Aesthetics*, ed. Michael Kelly, 2nd ed. (Oxford: Oxford University Press, 2014), http://www.oxfordreference.com/view/10.1093/acref/9780199747108.001.0001/acref-9780199747108-e-575.

158 Austin, "More to See than a Canvas in a White Cube."

159 Austin, 42.

160 Austin, 37–40. On street art's challenge against Modern separation of art and life, see also Baldini, "Street Art: A Reply to Riggle"; Nicholas Alden Riggle, "Street Art: The Transfiguration of the Commonplaces," *The Journal of Aesthetics and Art Criticism* 68, no. 3 (2010): 243–57.

161 Baldini, "Street Art: A Reply to Riggle," 189–90.

Commodification in art has been a central concern for many artists – at least – for the last fifty years. A key motivation that many performance artists shared, for instance, has been to produce art resisting commercial exploitations and its reduction to a market product exchanged for money.[162] Rather than focusing on the living body as a way to escape the logic of the art market, street artists sabotage the fundamental institution at the very foundation of financial economies, that is, private property. By rejecting this cornerstone of capitalist society, street art embodies "an economy of the 'gift'," as Michel de Certeau would say, an economy that stands outside the pale of profit.[163] In this sense, street art's vandalism – by ignoring the foundation of market economy, that is, private property – functions as an effective tool to achieve this rejection of commodification.[164]

As an aesthetic-political creative practice, street art's significance transcends the artistic domain, even when broadly construed. Examples of this urban art kind produce a political impact that one should not ignore or downplay. As I have already mentioned, one could identify the political significance of street art by its capacity of challenging dominant hierarchies of visibility, which favor commercial communication over all other forms of expression in the city. Street art opposes this monopoly. Such a political 'mission,' of which street artists are not always fully aware, is often carried out through the use of vandalism. As the French street artist Invader writes, "The way I [Invader] operate is per se already political as I intervene illegally for 99% of my installation" (fig. 5).[165]

At this point, one might ask why I claim that vandalism is an artistic technique rather than the other way around. In other words, why isn't the artistic quality of street art a tool for vandalism? I think that we can offer to this question a rather straightforward answer, which can help us further illuminate the nature of this urban art kind and its relationship with the law. Street artists' primary goal is not to violate the law. In spite of mentioning a certain carnivalesque *jouissance* as a powerful motivator, street artists of all sorts and varieties – even the most radical ones such as graffiti writers – are concerned

162 For a seminal analysis of performance art, see Amelia Jones, *Body Art/Performing the Subject* (Minneapolis; London: University of Minnesota Press, 1998).

163 de Certeau, *The Practice of Everyday Life*, 27. See also Irvine, "The Work on the Street," 252.

164 Especially after Marina Abramovic's 2010 retrospective at the MOMA *The Artist is Present*, it is controversial whether performance art has been successful in escaping commodification. In a similar vein, recent controversies of street art appropriation and street artists' copyrights and moral rights raise similar doubts about the anti-commercial nature of this urban art kind. Chapter 3 addresses this issue.

165 "Invader – About," accessed February 7, 2016, http://www.space-invaders.com/about/.

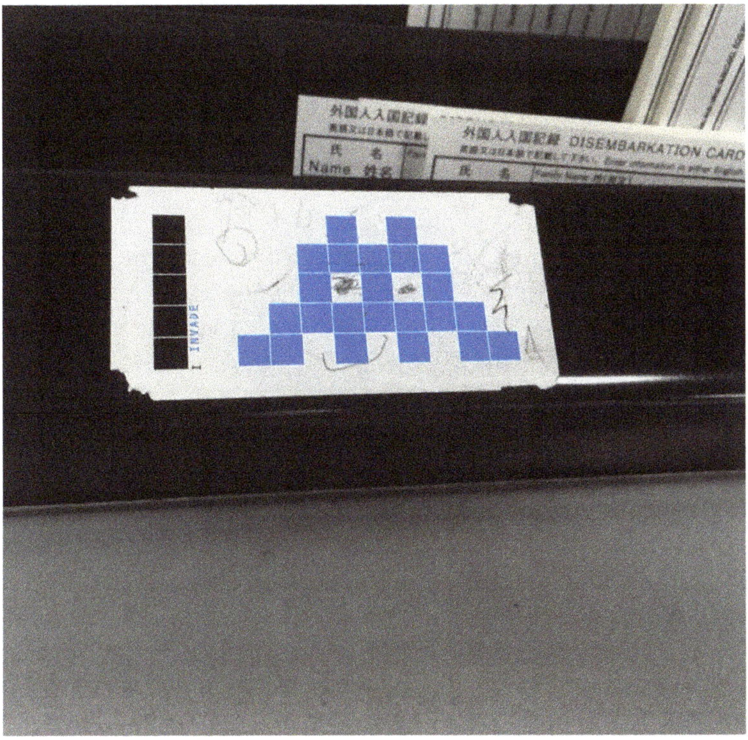


FIGURE 5 Sticker by Invader at the customs of Tokyo Airport
PHOTOGRAPH TAKEN BY THE AUTHOR

with style, form, techniques, and how to use them as a means to create content and to deliver a message. Street art is a practice of meaning-making that exploits, among other things, vandalism as a tool for materializing a particular idea. Its goal is not purely destructive or a mere juvenile rejection of authority. Street art does more than that: in refusing to comply with the status quo, it wants to tell us something.

Let me add at this point an important consequence of my characterization of the relationship between street art and vandalism. The vandalism question (and the exclusive disjunction that it implies) is not merely a conceptual non-starter. It is also a move which raises artistic concerns. If realized, it would possibly turn (all forms of) art into something politically inert.[166] Even in the unlikely case that one could come up with a plausible way to construe the dualism of 'art or vandalism,' this would eventually contribute to the insulation of street art (and the arts in general) from other domains of human action. In effect, as

166 For a more detailed discussion of this point, see Baldini, "Beauty and the Behest."

the civil rights movements, for instance, have shown us, violating laws that one considers unjust is a powerful tool of social and political protest. Denying this possibility to the arts is to reduce them to mere form of decoration and to deny that "continuity between the [...] works of art and the everyday events, doings, and sufferings" that, among others, John Dewey rightly emphasized and praised.[167]

Is it art or vandalism? In this chapter, I addressed this general question, which I called the vandalism question. This interrogative has attracted much attention from theorists as well as lay persons discussing forms of street art since the emergence of modern graffiti. I developed an analysis of the assumptions that ground the vandalism question and argued that the exclusive disjunction that it implies cannot be meaningfully construed. The binary opposition between art and the law cannot be vindicated within the context of street art. As a consequence of this recognition, I suggested that we discard the vandalism question and proposed to instead look at street art as an aesthetic-political practice that is both art and vandalism. In specifying the connection between these two sides of street art, I characterized vandalism as an artistic tool, technique, or resource informing the production and experience of street art that practitioners use to challenge the Modern separation of art and life, and artistic commodification. In the following chapter, I will expand the discussion of the relationship between street artworks and commodities by considering issues of private property, copyright, and commercial exploitation framed in terms of following question: Who owns street art?

## Part 3. Creativity, Profit, and Commercial Exploitation: Should Property Rights Extend to Street Art?

### 1 *Introduction*

In the last few years, prominent street artists have filed a series of high profile lawsuits against international corporations and real estate developers. Some cases challenged violations of copyright privileges that occur when appropriating a street artist's design for marketing purposes or for developing commercial products. In other judicial litigations, street artists denounced the violation of their moral rights for the destruction of their works. These lawsuits have drawn the spotlight to some significant as well as controversial aspects of the relationship between street art and the law. These aspects are related to

167 John Dewey, *Art as Experience* (New York: Perigee Books, 1980), 3.

issues of property rights, copyright, and moral rights, which have since then become a key topic of discussion both in general media and specialized circles.

Recently, a dominant trend has emerged among commentators both inside and outside of academia. There seems to be a growing consensus of opinions that favor the extension of copyright privileges and moral rights to street art. Many warmly welcome this development as intrinsically positive. To borrow the words of Sonia Rao, including street art under the copyright umbrella shows that this art kind has finally be "taken seriously."[168] With that said, it is still unclear whether this optimism is justified, and whether this trajectory is a positive turn in the history of street art or rather its end. Admitting that it is legally possible, why should the law extend copyright and moral rights to street art? Call this the *justification question.*

This chapter considers the justification question and some of its implications. I cast doubts on the optimism about extending copyright and moral rights to street art. The main concern which is feeding my skepticism is the following: such an extension puts the subversive nature of this urban art kind at risk. Rather than protecting or promoting its value, asking for copyright and moral rights protection may very well contribute to the disappearance of street art insofar as it favors its commodification and absorption within mainstream art.

In spite of my skepticism, I nonetheless agree that something should be done to safeguard street art from corporate appropriation. I look at the literature on copynorms and the trajectory of the Creative Commons as a better way to find a satisfactory balance between protecting street art's subversiveness and preventing its commercial exploitation.

## 2 *Walls and Ownership: a Review of Current Literature on Street Art and Proprietary Rights*

Most discussions on proprietary rights in the context of street art have been carried out by scholars working in legal studies, in particular within the American and British contexts, that are the focus of my discussion.[169] Much of what

168 Sonia Rao, "H&M's Battle with the Artist Revok Shows How Street Art Is Being Taken Seriously," *Washington Post,* March 16, 2018, https://www.washingtonpost.com/news/arts-and-entertainment/wp/2018/03/16/hms-battle-with-the-artist-revok-shows-how-street-art-is-being-taken-seriously/.

169 See, among others, Bonadio, "Copyright Protection of Street Art and Graffiti under UK Law"; Lucy Finchett-Maddock, "In Vacuums of Law We Find: Outsider Poiesis in Street Art and Graffiti," SSRN Scholarly Paper (Rochester, NY: Social Science Research Network, 2017), https://papers.ssrn.com/abstract=3066309; Marta Iljadica, "Graffiti and the Moral Right of Integrity," *Intellectual Property Quarterly* 3 (2015): 266–88; Marta Iljadica, "Street

one can read about this issue has to do with the applicability of current legislations dealing with such rights to cases of street art. In this sense, rather than focus on the justification question, recent scholarship has been focusing on the following first order question about proprietary rights and street art: Given the current laws, should proprietary rights apply to street art?

When asking this question, one is generally interested in understanding who owns (or has some kind of proprietary rights over) either one of the two following aspects of a street artwork: the tangible support and the intangible work.[170] First, when clarifying the exact nature of proprietary rights over a street artwork's tangible medium, one wants to know who owns the physical objects that street artists use as the physical support for their creations. In other words, one is concerned with the ownership of the particular that possesses those physical (and perceptual) properties and that is the outcome of a street artist's creativity. These discussions take then as their focus rights of ownership.

Before starting to review previous studies, let me briefly introduce the notion of creativity that I use here. In a basic sense, creativity "involves coming up with a surprising, valuable idea that's new *to the person who comes up with it*."[171] Margaret Boden calls this ability "P-creativity" (or psychological creativity). In some occasions, a person creates an artefact or comes up with an idea that no one else had done or thought before: something "has risen for the first time in human history."[172] By following Boden, we can identify this ability as "H-creativity" (or historical creativity). H-creativity is a special case of P-creativity. All instances of H-creativity are instances of P-creativity, but the converse does not hold. Though copyright as well as common sense tend to

---

Art Belongs to the Freeholder," *Journal of Intellectual Property Law & Practice* 11, no. 2 (2016): 90–91, https://doi.org/10.1093/jiplp/jpv230; Marta Iljadica, *Copyright Beyond Law: Regulating Creativity in the Graffiti Subculture* (London: Bloomsbury Publishing, 2016); Margaret L. Mettler, "Graffiti Museum: A First Amendment Argument for Protecting Uncommissioned Art on Private Property," *Michigan Law Review* 111, no. 2 (2012): 249–81; Peter N. Salib, "The Law of Banksy: Who Owns Street Art?," *The University of Chicago Law Review* 82, no. 4 (2015): 2293–2328.

170 The distinction between tangible medium and intangible work finds an interesting parallel in discussions about the distinction between physical- and meaning-properties of an artwork. For two influential and opposing views on this aspect of artworks' metaphysics, see, for instance, Danto, *The Transfiguration of the Commonplace*; Joseph Margolis, *What, After All, Is a Work of Art?: Lectures in the Philosophy of Art* (University Park, PA: Pennsylvania State University Press, 1999).

171 Margaret A. Boden, *Creativity and Art: Three Roads to Surprise* (Oxford: Oxford University Press, 2010), 30. Emphasis in the original.

172 Boden, 30.

favor H-creativity, P-creativity is also a genuine form of creativity. This distinction will help me explain and unpack the issue of street art and copyright.

Let us now return to reviewing the literature. Among discussions of proprietary rights and street art, disputes about the correct legal interpretation of ownership rights over the tangible medium are the least controversial. Judicially, the issue appears rather settled. The case *Creative Foundation v Dreamland & Others* provides us with a clear precedent on the matter.[173] As Enrico Bonadio emphasizes, this sentence provides legal evidence in favor of the following view: "the ownership of the tangible medium where the work is placed (a wall, a train car, a litter bin, etc.) will obviously remain with the property owner."[174] This is far from an extraordinary fact. In effect, this "is also the case with traditional works of art, such as paintings," Bonadio rightly adds, where "the buyer of the painting acquires a property title over the object."[175] In other words, if a street artist realizes a stencil-graffiti on one of the outside walls of my house (which I legally own), the tangible object that the artist has realized becomes my property.

Second, let us consider the intangible work. Things are more complicated when dealing with this second aspect of a street artwork. When talking about the intangible work, one is generally referring to the meaning-structure or idea that the tangible support embodies or exemplifies. In other words, the intangible work refers to all those features that a street artwork possesses as a creation of human intellect and creativity. Discussions about proprietary rights over the intangible work primarily have to do with copyright and moral rights.

I shall begin by first examining copyright and street art. Some of the most prominent recent legal cases about street art are lawsuits concerning copyright violations.[176] As Lucy Finchett-Maddock emphasizes, so far, most of these

173 Creative Foundation v Dreamland Leisure Ltd [2015] EWHC 2556 (Ch) (September 11, 2015). One can find discussions of this case also in Bonadio, "Copyright Protection of Street Art and Graffiti under UK Law," 14; and, Iljadica, "Street Art Belongs to the Freeholder," 90.

174 Bonadio, "Copyright Protection of Street Art and Graffiti under UK Law," 13–14.

175 Bonadio, 14.

176 For instance, see "Oakley Denies Validity of Graffiti Copyright," *HYPEBEAST*, accessed June 25, 2018, https://hypebeast.com/2018/6/oakley-denies-validity-of-graffiti-copyright; "Another Graffiti Copyright Claim against a Major Brand – Robbins v Oakley," accessed June 25, 2018, http://uspatentlaw.cn/en/another-graffiti-copyright-claim-against-a-major-brand-robbins-v-oakley/; "Oakley Claims Artists' Graffiti Is Too 'Generic' to Be Copyrighted," *Artsy*, June 14, 2018, https://www.artsy.net/news/artsy-editorial-two-graffiti-artists-sued-oakley-clothing-brand-work-ads-permission; Alyssa Buffenstein, "Did McDonald's Steal Dash Snow's Grafitti Tag?," *artnet News*, October 5, 2016, https://news.artnet.com/art-world/dash-snows-family-sues-mcdonalds-copyright-infringement

cases have been settled out of court thus "leaving the question of whether [these] works can be protected under copyright as yet unsettled in law and open for interpretation by the intellectual property community."[177] We are then here in the domain of legal speculation, and what one can detect are general jurisprudential trajectories rather than definitive answers.

In spite of this general uncertainty, prominent scholars such as Bonadio and Marta Iljadica independently argue for the legal possibility of an extension of copyright to street art, even in cases of illegal works.[178] There are two necessary and sufficient conditions that a particular artifact must satisfy in order to fall under the privileges provided by copyright protection laws. Creators must establish that their works are: (i) original; and, (ii) "fixed," as described for instance in the title 17 of the U.S. Code, section 102, "in a tangible medium of expression." Let me consider these two requirements separately.

Some have suggested that most street artworks (and in particular basic forms of graffiti such as throw ups and tags) do not fulfil the originality requirement. For instance, legal representatives of Luxottica – the parent company of eyewear brand Oakley – responded with this argument to KEPTIONE's and DJ RAKUS's lawsuit.[179] On June 9, 2018, attorney Jeff Gluck filed a lawsuit on behalf of graffiti artists Donald Robbins and Noah Daar, whose street names are respectively KEPTIONE and DJ RAKUS, against the eyewear brand Oakley for copyright infringement.[180] A work produced by those two writers appeared in Oakley's new ad campaign. For Luxottica's legal team, as mere assemblages of simple colors, lines, and shapes, examples of graffiti lack that minimum degree of creativity required for copyright protection.

---

-685901; "Dash Snow," *Artnet* (blog), accessed July 1, 2018, http://www.artnet.com/artists/dash-snow/; Rao, "H&M's Battle with the Artist Revok Shows How Street Art Is Being Taken Seriously"; "UPDATE: Artists Revok, Reyes and Steel Are Suing Roberto Cavalli for Copyright Infringement," *HYPEBEAST*, accessed May 1, 2018, https://hypebeast.com/2015/2/artists-revok-reyes-and-steel-are-suing-roberto-cavalli-for-copyright-infringement; Scarlett Kilcooley-O'Halloran, "Cavalli's Graffiti War Wages On," *British Vogue*, accessed May 1, 2018, http://www.vogue.co.uk/article/graffiti-artists-respond-roberto-cavalli-lawsuit; "Graffiti Artists Sue Cavalli," *Widewalls*, accessed May 1, 2018, https://www.widewalls.ch/graffiti-artists-sue-cavalli.

177 Finchett-Maddock, "In Vacuums of Law We Find," 10.

178 Bonadio, "Copyright Protection of Street Art and Graffiti under UK Law"; Iljadica, "Graffiti and the Moral Right of Integrity"; Iljadica, "Street Art Belongs to the Freeholder"; Iljadica, *Copyright Beyond Law*.

179 "Oakley Denies Validity of Graffiti Copyright."

180 Robbins et al v. Oakley, Inc. et al, 2:18-cv-05116 (2018). See also, "Oakley Denies Validity of Graffiti Copyright"; "Another Graffiti Copyright Claim against a Major Brand – Robbins v Oakley"; "Oakley Claims Artists' Graffiti Is Too 'Generic' to Be Copyrighted."

However, denying street art's originality seems to be grounded on a misleading understanding of this legal requirement.[181] The law does not define originality in terms of artistic quality, inventiveness, or aesthetic merit.[182] A tangible work fulfils the originality requirement if it is independently created by its author, who must not have copied it from somebody else's work. If we were to borrow Boden's terminology, one could say that the originality requirement requires that, in order to be copyrightable, a tangible work *w* is an instance of H-creativity. It is irrelevant whether *w* is aesthetically or artistically worthless. It is enough that one has realized something without copying it from the work of someone else. Therefore, many examples of street art – even in the most basic form of graffiti, that is, tags and throw-ups – seem to meet the originality requirement.[183]

Let us consider the fixation requirement. One might think that the "commitment to *ephemerality*" that generally characterizes street art may prevent an extension of copyright protection to this artform's examples.[184] However, from a legal standpoint, there are good reasons to admit that works of street art fulfil the fixation requirement. This requirement simply wants to exclude the possibility of copyrighting ideas or facts that did not find realization in something tangible. However, when those ideas and facts are transformed into a concrete expression, we have something that is legally sheltered according to copyright laws: the product. The ontological persistence of such a product is irrelevant, as long as it acquired a tangible form at some point. The ruling of the case *Metix Ltd. v G.H. Maughan* provides evidence for the claim that even transient artworks are copyrightable.[185] The judge in effect accepted in principle the copyrightability of an ice sculpture, which is by far more ontologically precarious than most street artworks. Moreover, the material ephemerality of street art is not intrinsic, Bonadio maintains, but is rather a consequence of the peculiar conditions of their location or (illegal) circumstances of creation.[186]

181 Bonadio, "Copyright Protection of Street Art and Graffiti under UK Law," 7–10; Iljadica, "Street Art Belongs to the Freeholder," 91; Iljadica, *Copyright Beyond Law*, chap. 6.

182 Within the context of copyright protection, appeals to originality have been used, for instance, to exclude things like telephone books from copyright protection. See, for instance, Feist Publications, Inc., v. Rural Telephone Service Co., No. 499 U.S. 340 (1991).

183 Bonadio, "Copyright Protection of Street Art and Graffiti under UK Law," 8.

184 Riggle, "Street Art: The Transfiguration of the Commonplaces," 245. Emphasis in the original.

185 Metix (UK) Ltd v G H Maughan (Plastics) Ltd, No. FSR 718 (1997). See also Bonadio, "Copyright Protection of Street Art and Graffiti under UK Law," 6.

186 Bonadio, "Copyright Protection of Street Art and Graffiti under UK Law," 6; Iljadica, *Copyright Beyond Law*, 99–108.

Street artists in general create products that have tangible nature, and therefore fulfil the fixation requirement.

Some have also questioned the applicability of copyright to a significant subset of street artworks, that is, illegal street artworks, on the basis of the so-called *unclean hands doctrine*.[187] This doctrine embodies the principle that parties seeking justice or relief must show that their conduct, insofar as it concerns the particular controversy relevant to discussion, has also been fair, honest, and equitable. Recently, H&M has used this line of reasoning during their initial rejection of REVOK's accusation of wrongfully including one of his iconic illegal pieces in one of the Swedish clothing brand's recent ad campaigns.[188] Asking for copyright privileges to protect a vandalistic action seems to be in plain violation of this principle.

The lack of significant legal precedents in the UK and the USA makes the discussion of the applicability of the unclean hands doctrine rather speculative in these contexts (and in others, as well). However, Bonadio and Iljiadica have offered independent arguments in favor of the view that copyright protects illegal street artworks. Bonadio develops two justifications in favor of such a view. The first one is an argument from analogy. It starts with a hypothetical case of an artist drawing a masterpiece with a stolen pencil. It seems absurd, Bonadio maintains, to claim that the artist does not have copyright over the artwork just because of the stolen pencil. The second one is an argument from fairness.[189] "It would indeed be unfair," Bonadio writes, "to allow persons other than the artist to rely on the illegal nature of a street artwork to copy and exploit it for their own commercial purposes".[190] Iljadica cites two cases, one from Germany and the other one from France, showing that, even in cases of illegal street artworks, owners of the tangible medium cannot exploit the copyright of the intangible work in the absence of the street artist's consent.[191] These arguments seem then to provide at least some evidence for the view that copyright privileges also apply to illegal street art, and that the unclean hands doctrine need not apply to at least some of those cases.

---

187 For a recent discussion of the "unclean hands" doctrine, see among others T. Leigh Anenson, "Limiting Legal Remedies: An Analysis of Unclean Hands," *Kentucky Law Journal* 99 (2011): 63–118.

188 Rao, "H&M's Battle with the Artist Revok Shows How Street Art Is Being Taken Seriously." H&M has since then abandoned the case against REVOK. See "H&M VS Jason Revok Williams and the Problem of Street Art," *nss magazine*, accessed July 27, 2018, https://www.nssmag.com/en/article/14226.

189 For a view echoing Bonadio's argument from fairness, see also Iljadica, *Copyright Beyond Law*, 107.

190 Bonadio, "Copyright Protection of Street Art and Graffiti under UK Law," 35.

191 Iljadica, *Copyright Beyond Law*, 107.

Even when considering the relationship between moral rights and street art, opinions and interpretations are contested and controversial. Moral rights, which generally apply to works protected by copyright, are special rights that authors possess over their respective creations as a consequence of the special relationship connecting creators and their own creations.[192] Moral rights include, among others, the rights of attribution and integrity, which are the focus of this discussion.

The right of attribution allows "authors to claim to be recognised as the creators of their works."[193] In cases of signed works, Bonadio believes that street artists can claim paternity – even when using a pseudonym. If operating anonymously, that is, without signaling either their actual or street identities, street artists cannot assert their right of attribution in some systems of law, such as the British one.[194]

The extension of the right of integrity to street art finds an important legal precedent in the recent ruling about works installed at the 5Pointz site in New York. Street artists who created some of their works at this notorious cultural space with the authorization of the building owner turned to the law as a way to protect their works from destruction. Initially, artists failed to stop the redevelopment of the area, and their works were destroyed.[195] However, in 2018, the judge awarded $6.7 million as a compensation for the whitewashing of the murals.[196] This historic ruling first established that street artworks – including graffiti writing – can be of 'recognized stature,' which is a necessary condition for appeals to the right of integrity.

In cases of unauthorized installation of street artworks on public and private property, things are different. As Ilijadica stresses, as "the US case *English v BFC* indicates, works placed without permission are even less likely to fare well."[197] In the ruling, the court maintains that "moral rights statute applied only to 'art that is affixed or attached by arrangement with the owner' [as in the case of 5Pointz] for otherwise parties could effectively freeze development

192 For a discussion of moral rights in American law, see Edward J. Damich, "A Critique of the Visual Artists Rights Act of 1989," *Nova Law Review* 14, no. 2 (1990): 407–20.

193 Bonadio, "Copyright Protection of Street Art and Graffiti under UK Law," 15.

194 Bonadio, 15.

195 Iljadica, *Copyright Beyond Law*, 231.

196 Cohen v G & M Realty L.P. (EDNY 2013 / 2018). See also Feuer, "Graffiti Artists Awarded $6.7 Million for Destroyed 5Pointz Murals"; Associated Press, "5Pointz Graffiti Artists Awarded $6.7m in Lawsuit after Renowned Work Torn Down," *The Guardian*, February 13, 2018, sec. US news, http://www.theguardian.com/us-news/2018/feb/12/graffiti-artists-5pointz-lawsuit.

197 Iljadica, *Copyright Beyond Law*, 231.

of vacant lots by placing artwork there without permission."[198] In this sense, scholars generally agree that, when street artworks are not commissioned or unauthorized, the rights of property owners should supersede those of artists.[199]

In this section, I have reviewed recent legal scholarship on proprietary rights within the context of street art. The list of judicial precedents is expanding, and the theoretical interest from scholars is growing. However, it is still unclear how the law should handle controversies of street art dealing with copyright and moral rights protection. In the following section, I turn to considering the justification question.

## 3 *Copyright and Street Art: the Creativity Argument*

As we have seen, legal scholars are currently debating whether, under current legislations, copyright and moral rights can extend to cases of street art. However, a different and more fundamental question asks whether we should extend copyright and moral rights to street art. I have called this interrogation the justification question. This is, of course, a second-order question of philosophical import, a question that cuts through the technical discussions of legal merits of copyright and moral rights claims in current judicial practices. The answer to the justification question aims at unpacking possible motivations that ground a desire to extend copyright and moral rights to street art.

My primary motive for looking into the justification question is the following: lawsuits involving considerations of street art and proprietary rights are generally *hard cases*.[200] As Gregory Keating has aptly described them, "Hard cases arise when the law's stock of settled rules and rulings is insufficient to resolve a dispute".[201] Such an incapacity of providing apt legal solutions may depend on conflicts among rules and the resulting competing answers, or it may depend on a lack of normative tools for handling those cases.

Hard cases require judgments based on philosophically and theoretically more basic considerations. These cases call for evaluations that refer back to a society's founding moral principles. "Such cases," Keating writes, "force judges to reconstruct the fabric of moral – and one could add also political, social,

---

198 English v BFC 1999 US App LEXIS 35242 11. Also cited in Iljadica, 231.

199 Bonadio, "Copyright Protection of Street Art and Graffiti under UK Law," 19; Jamie Griffin, "Illegal Graffiti: A Copyright Perspective," *Intellectual Property Law Bulletin* 20 (2010): 124.

200 For a classic discussion of hard cases, see Ronald Dworkin, *Law's Empire* (Cambridge, MA: Belknap Press, 1986).

201 Gregory C. Keating, "Justifying Hercules: Ronald Dworkin and the Rule of Law," *American Bar Foundation Research Journal* (1987): 526.

cultural, etc. – principles which underpins the law's black-letter rules and doctrines and to fashion out of that fabric a new and purer vision of what the law might be."[202] Answering the justification question can thus help us gain clarity about those moral values motivating the extension of laws that regulate proprietary issues of street art.

This section begins to address possible justifications for extending copyright privileges to street art. However, for the sake of explanatory completeness, let me first quickly consider justification of an application of proprietary rights to street art. As we have already seen, current legislations generally accept that individuals, companies, or organizations owning a building, a train car, a wall, or whatever support a street artist used to create a work are also entitled to own the tangible medium. In these cases, an extension of current laws regulating private and public property to cases of street art seems reasonable. Street artists may very well question our current hierarchy and understanding of public and private property, as legendary graffiti writers Utah and Ether certainly do.[203] However, I have no knowledge of street artists reclaiming property over the tangible media that they have used to create their respective works. This view would require an explicit argument, which I do not see. It just sounds too extreme to be reasonable. The direction that the law is following here thus seems to be justified.

Let us now turn to a justification of an extension of copyright to street art. Why should we extend copyright to street art? Contrary to a commonsensical view that is picking up momentum, I do not see any self-evident answer to this question. In particular, I do not equate the rise of street art to the status of copyrightable material in terms of a recognition of its value. Street art was "taken seriously" even before the law started to recognize copyright privileges to its practitioners.[204] I am sympathetic with scholars who cast doubts on the idea that copyright is the gold standard of cultural and intellectual value.[205]

As a way to provide evidence for my unpopular – and yet, I believe, correct – view, I opt for the following strategy. I consider, in turn, moral justifications of extending copyright and moral rights privileges to street art, and I will

---

202 Keating, 527.

203 "Exclusive Interview with Utah & Ether, Graffiti's Bonnie & Clyde," *The Hundreds*, accessed May 11, 2017, https://thehundreds.com/blogs/content/utah-ether-interview.

204 Rao, "H&M's Battle with the Artist Revok Shows How Street Art Is Being Taken Seriously."

205 Kristopher Pitzek, "Copyright Law and the Democraticization of Cultural Value," *Global Societies Journal* 1, no. 1 (2013), https://escholarship.org/uc/item/9dr224z3; Siva Vaidhyanathan, *Copyrights and Copywrongs: The Rise of Intellectual Property and How It Threatens Creativity* (New York: New York University Press, 2001).

show their limitations. Before I start the *pars destruens* of my argument, let me add one point. My view differs from other scholars who are similarly critical of street art copyrightability in the following way: I recognize that street art – and the world – is changing.[206] We cannot pretend that we are in the old days of graffiti. Something needs to be done, because the rising popularity of street art requires this of us. Ignoring this simple fact is to passively accept whatever will come. I am also dissatisfied with this possibility. Therefore, in the *pars costruens* of my argument, I suggest how we should handle copyright and moral rights issues in the context of street art.

The most common strategy for defending copyright privileges appeals to these laws' capacity to foster and promote creativity. "Copyright law," Evan Brown suggests, "in general is usually justified as incentivizing production of expressive works, often for public consumption."[207] One could then reconstruct this justification as follows. Copyright provides artists with privileges that allow them to protect and profit (both in terms of economic return and cultural recognition) from their works. This in turn fosters artistic activities by promoting overall creativity, which in turn enriches our lives. As such, copyright seems morally justifiable as a piece of legislation aimed at cultivating public good. Call this the *creativity argument*.

The creativity argument has been already questioned from different disciplinary perspectives.[208] Moreover, when we look at the practice of street art, one cannot fail to notice how weak – to put it mildly – this argument is. The practice of street art is perhaps the most powerful counterexample to the creativity argument. Since graffiti writing emerged in the 1960s, street artists – of which writers are the original and most radical practitioners – have inundated trains, walls, and even the smallest cracks of our cities with their works in the complete absence of any legal sheltering of their creativity: no profit, no protection, no privileges were awarded by the law. Even if for some artists mainstream cultural recognition and profit may very well be powerful motivators, they are far from necessary.

206 For works from critical voices about the extension of copyright and moral rights to street art, see Samuel Merrill, "Keeping It Real? Subcultural Graffiti, Street Art, Heritage and Authenticity," *International Journal of Heritage Studies* 21, no. 4 (2015): 369–89, https://doi.org/10.1080/13527258.2014.934902; Finchett-Maddock, "In Vacuums of Law We Find."

207 See, among others, Evan Brown, "Fixed Perspectives: The Evolving Contours of the Fixation Requirement in Copyright Law," *Washington Journal of Law, Technology & Arts* 10 (2014): 33; Vaidhyanathan, *Copyrights and Copywrongs*.

208 Brown, "Fixed Perspectives."

By pressing the point, one could also add that, arguably, street art is one of the most relevant forms of artistic expression that emerged in the last fifty years or so – if not the most important of the last two decades. As Joe Austin correctly claims, street art "is a significant contribution to, even a step forward for, modern art."[209] The progress in this field, if I may use this word, happened outside the oversight of copyright legislation. This could be considered as a hint in favor of the following view: Copyright legislation is an inhibitor rather than a promoter of creativity.[210] The ever-expanding control that copyright exercises on artistic creation is imposing limitations on our culture(s), limitations that are actually detrimental to free expression. By ignoring all of these restrictions, street artists have found a way to inject creativity into the city. An allegiance with copyright may very well revert this tendency and put street artists' inventiveness on a leash.

The suggestion that copyright inhibits rather than promoting creativity echoes Siva Vaidhyanathan's powerful criticism of intellectual property legislations.[211] In *Copyrights and Copywrongs*, he argues that copyright law favors conceptions of creativity that dominate mainstream Anglo-European cultural practices. The limits of copyright laws clearly appear when dealing with non-mainstream artistic genres. The following point is central to Vaidhyanathan's analysis: In practices that are not built around the notions of authorship and originality typical of Western fine arts, free borrowing and appropriation are often common and legitimate creative strategies. Copyright obviously does not allow for those tactics. In other words, copyright favors practices built around the notion of H-creativity, while disallowing and demoting those that are centered on the use of P-creativity. Therefore, such legislation is not a suitable instrument to protect and promote such practices.

Vaidhyanathan discusses the example of rap: Its artistic reliance on musical sampling and mixing, that is, of instances of P-creativity, challenges the notion of creativity that informs copyright law. "Rap," he writes, "revealed gaping flaws in the premises of how copyright law gets applied to music and shown the law to be inadequate for emerging communication technologies, techniques, and aesthetics."[212] What one could find valuable and original in rap music was – among other things – a constant legal trespass in terms of copyright law.

---

209 Austin, "More to See than a Canvas in a White Cube," 42.

210 For a systematic discussion of a worry about copyright as an inhibitor of creativity, see Lawrence Lessig, *The Future of Ideas: The Fate of the Commons in a Connected World* (New York: Random House, 2001).

211 Vaidhyanathan, *Copyrights and Copywrongs*.

212 Vaidhyanathan, 133.

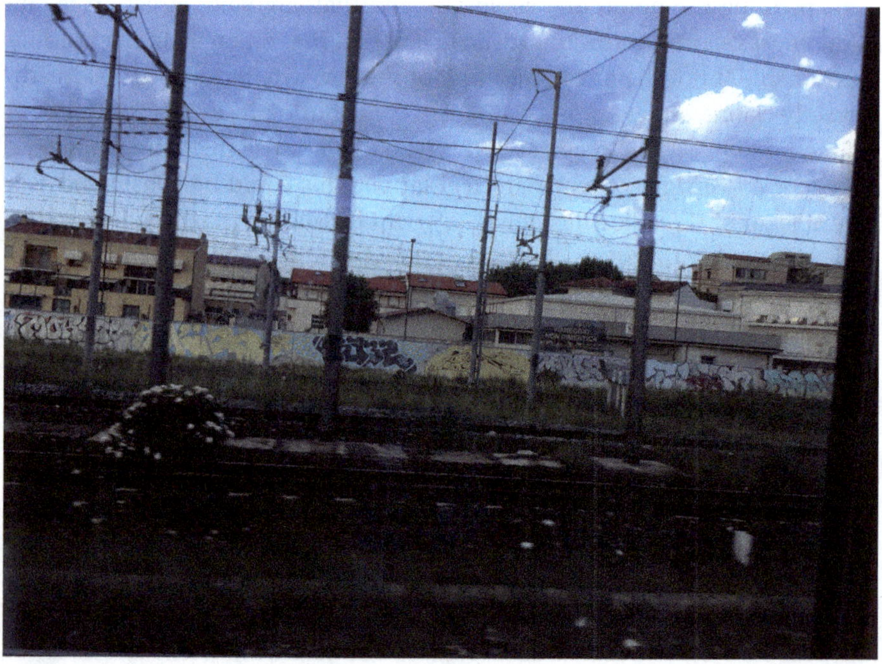

FIGURE 6 A photo of the walls in the vicinity of Viareggio's train station taken from inside the train
PHOTOGRAPH TAKEN BY THE AUTHOR

Something similar happens in street art: the notion of creativity that structures this urban art kind deeply relies on borrowing and appropriation. It is surely grounded on P-creativity rather than on H-creativity. The most famous case is perhaps that of Banksy and Blek le Rat. Banksy explicitly admits borrowing and appropriating from Blek's work.[213] But this is also evident in regional schools of graffiti writing. When traveling through the coast of Tuscany, from Viareggio to Livorno and beyond, one can see hundreds of examples of graffiti that unequivocally borrow from the style of legendary writer Fra32 (fig. 6). The reason why this is the case is simple: Before moving to Australia, Fra32 directly shaped the styles of his crew and affiliates.[214] As a tribute to his fame, some writers close to Fra32, such as SAME and RIE, have also painted pieces that borrow not only his style, but also his signature (fig. 7). In graffiti writing, as well as in other forms of street art, borrowing and appropriation are surely forms of appreciation and tribute informing the creative acts of street artists.

213 Garry Hunter, *Street Art: From Around the World* (London: Arcturus Publishing, 2013), 16.
214 Domenico De Girolamo and Andrew Dale, *Glorious Attitude / Fra32* (Rome: Whole Train Press, 2018).

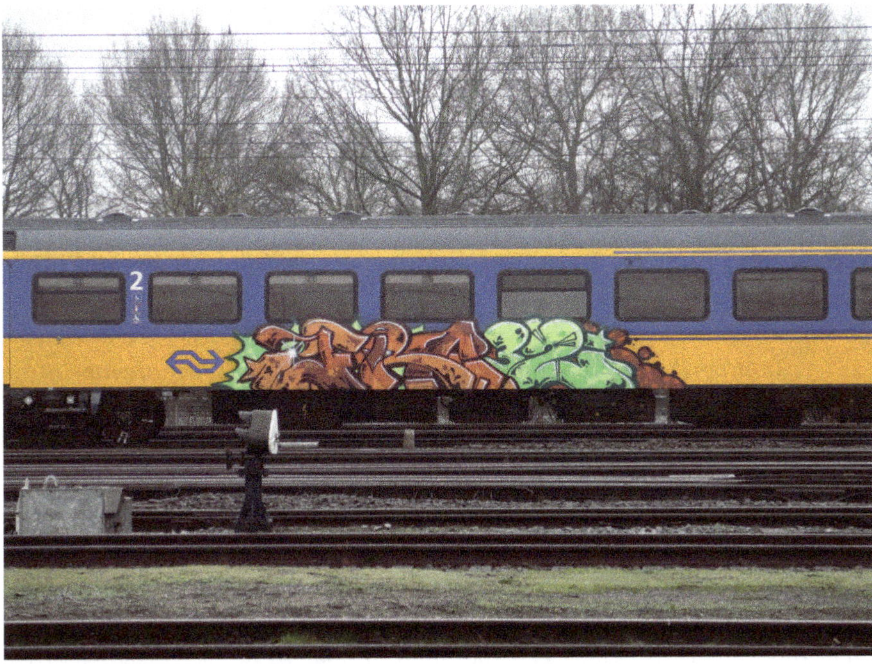

FIGURE 7 A tribute to Fra32 by SAME painted on a train in the Netherlands
PHOTOGRAPH COURTESY OF FRA32

P-creativity, in other words, is not disparaged as theft, but is seen as a grounding principle of the practice related to this art kind.

As in the case of rap, copyright law does not accommodate this non-mainstream understanding of creativity as P-creativity, which is often based on borrowing and appropriation, in an acceptable manner. P-creativity significantly informs practices related to street art as an art kind. The risk that we are facing in pushing for the extension of copyright to street artworks is that of actively suppressing alternative forms of expression, that is, to inhibit instances of P-creativity that animates the life of this art kind. Copyright could profoundly have an impact on street art and its modes of expression.

Contrary to what Bonadio claims, we cannot rely on street artists' general reluctance to take legal action against peers that may have infringed copyright privileges, for instance, by appropriating their design. This hope cannot guarantee that the practice will not perish under this form of legal institutionalization.[215]

215 Bonadio, "Copyright Protection of Street Art and Graffiti under UK Law," 36–37.

If extending copyright to street art is meant to provide a commitment to foster creativity in general, that is, P-creativity, then such a justification seems to fail. Copyright primarily promotes only a certain variety of creativity, that is, H-creativity, and cannot protect street art without irremediably transforming it into something different. If we value the rogue form of creativity that street art embodies based on appropriation and borrowing, we should be very careful before extending copyright privileges to this art form. In the following section, I turn to two alternative arguments justifying an extension of copyright privileges to street art.

## 4 *Another Pass at Copyrighting Street Art: Bonadio's Arguments*

In his work on street art and the law, Bonadio primarily focuses on examining current copyright legislations and their applicability to legal controversies of street art. However, he also briefly, though pertinently, addresses the justification question. He offers two arguments justifying the extension of copyright privileges to street art. Both of his defenses for applying copyright to street art significantly differ from the creativity argument, and therefore deserve attention.

Let us begin with what I call the *profit argument*. Bonadio suggests that "copyright could [...] serve as a means of commercial exploitation should artists decide to extract profits out of their activity and passion".[216] Copyright privileges, Bonadio then argues, can unleash commercial possibilities for street artists such as selling products inspired by their street style, which some have called "street art souvenirs" or "street art flavored" works.[217] Extensions of this variety of proprietary rights over the design of these products can thus help street artists generate revenue, which is – of course – a positive thing. The profit generated through these activities can support both street artists' everyday needs and their activities, including those spontaneous interventions in the streets that passersby can enjoy for free.

I generally agree with the profit argument. Only a hypocrite of the worst kind could dismiss *a priori* a strategy that street artists could adopt as a way to support themselves and pay their bills. Like virtually every other adult on the planet, artists need money to live their lives. However, the profit argument is *not* about street art in the proper sense. As Bonadio explicitly admits, this argument deals with commercial products derived from street art, but such objects are not street artworks *per se*. Therefore, how copyright deals with those objects need not bear on how we answer the justification question.

216 Bonadio, 38.
217 Bonadio, 38.

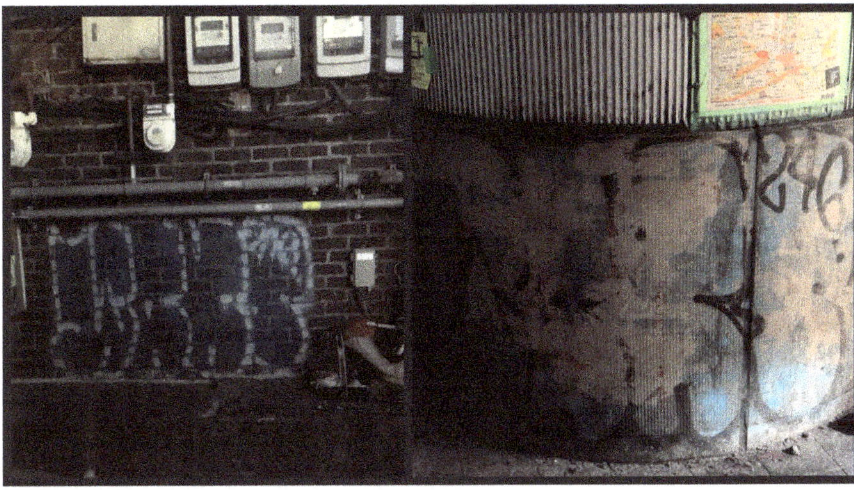

FIGURE 8 Two throw-ups by legendary Japanese writer WANTO in Seoul (left) and Tokyo (right)
PHOTOGRAPHS TAKEN BY THE AUTHOR

Many street artists sell their merchandise through authorized galleries and shops, or even have productions of artworks dedicated to a gallery and an auction circuit. In terms of this peculiar business, Shepard Fairey has been both a pioneer and a key figure. Among other things, he created a successful clothing line named after its street name, that is, OBEY. His commercial success has sometimes been seen as problematic for the street art status of his work.[218] However, many other street artists that are widely considered to be genuine expressions of the genre – such as Blu, MOSES and TAPS, Os Gemeos, Utah and Ether, and WANTO – are also involved in commercial businesses that they use to generate profit (fig. 8).[219] But products associated with these trading activities are not street art. How copyright deals with those objects has to do with how such rights regulate and influence commercial practices.

Bonadio's second argument justifies the extension of copyright privileges from a different – and perhaps more interesting – perspective. It argues that copyright can allow street artists to preserve the "anti-establishment" – or subversive – nature of their practice by providing them with the judicial tools

218 Riggle, "Street Art: The Transfiguration of the Commonplaces"; Baldini, "Street Art: A Reply to Riggle."

219 For an interesting discussion of a sample of street artists' strategies for self-support, see Jens Besser, "Cash for Chaos. Marketing, Self-Support, Bonds and Funding and in the Field of Trainpainting," in *1984: Evoluzione e Rigenerazione Del Writing*, ed. Pietro Rivasi (Modena: Galleria Civica di Modena, 2016), 26–27, Exhibition catalogue.

to oppose any commercial appropriation of their works and designs at the hands of big brands and corporations. In other words, copyright – Bonadio suggests – may very well serve in cases such as those of Dash Snow or REVOK to fight back against the commercial appropriation of street artworks for, among other things, advertisement or product design. Such an appropriation appears "antithetical to [the practice's anti-establishment] message."[220] This in turn can protect the reputation of street artists who generally refuse to be associated with those big companies. In this sense, copyright could be an instrument for preserving street art's subversive nature. Call this the *subversiveness argument*.

As a theorist who emphasizes the subversive nature of street art, in principle I cannot help but welcome all of these moves – including legal ones – that can be instrumental in protecting or fostering the dissident side of this urban art kind. However, I hasten to add, copyright *as it stands* is not the solution. Quite the opposite: Falling under the control of copyright seems to normalize the practice of street art, and to turn it into something institutional and commodified. Let me explain this point in more detail.

As was already discussed in previous chapters, one plausible way to understand street art's subversiveness is in terms of its capacity to turn upside down current norms and laws regulating the uses of visible surfaces in public spaces. Street art introduces profound discontinuities in the nature and uses of urban spaces, and transforms parts of the city into what activist Hakim Bey would call *temporary autonomous zones*.[221] There, the order imposed by the law is suspended, and people are free to express themselves in ways that are spontaneous, unrestricted, and not driven by profit. Thanks to the spatial transformation that it catalyzes, street art functions as a tactic for subverting dominant hierarchies of visibility and the status quo.

By expanding the analysis of street art in the light of Bey's temporary autonomous zones, one could interpret the activity of street artists as instances of "uprising."[222] For Bey, uprisings, which are often labeled "failed revolutions," are exceptional moments.[223] They are "peak" experiences that, in their temporariness, oppose "the standard of 'ordinary' consciousness" of our everyday

220 Bonadio, "Copyright Protection of Street Art and Graffiti under UK Law," 38.

221 Hakim Bey, *T.A.Z: The Temporary Autonomous Zone, Ontological Anarchy, Poetic Terrorism* (Boulder, CO: Wiretap; NetLibrary, 1991). See also Hakim Bey, "The Temporary Autonomous Zone," in *Crypto Anarchy, Cyberstates, and Pirate Utopias*, ed. Peter Ludlow (Cambridge, MA and London, UK: MIT Press, 2001), 401–34.

222 Bey, "The Temporary Autonomous Zone," 403.

223 Bey, 403.

life.[224] During those moments, which are necessarily short-lived like carnivals or festivals, one experiences an unconstrained autonomy that, for Bey, gives "meaning to the entirety of life."[225]

An appeal to copyright privileges seems to me an unlikely means to preserve and protect street art's anti-establishment and revolutionary nature. The first piece of evidence in favor of this dismissal is rather straightforward. Such an appeal, in effect, implies a recognition and an acknowledgement of the validity of those very rules that street art wants to put into question. It implies that street artists must accept the same authority that they mock, ridicule, and taunt.[226] When turning to copyright laws as tools for (supposedly) protecting their works, street artists are legitimizing that system of power that they aim at opposing: They are renouncing or limiting that unconstrained independence that is typical of the temporary autonomous zones. Lawsuits from street artists against international corporations for copyright infringement seem therefore paradoxical and contradictory.

At this point, one might object that what I am saying is too radical or abstract, and that there are actually movements of resistance using the law as a tool for fighting against big corporations. This is certainly the case of the anti-consumerist activist collective RTMark, an "anarcho-aesthetico-activist organization that funds and orchestrates acts of 'creative subversion'."[227] Such acts usually exploit privileges that laws afford to these financial groups in order to oppose them. In this sense, street artists could be using copyright as a tool to fight corporate power just like RTMark does: "They are fighting fire with fire," one might say.

Though in principle I admit that one can hijack the law and use it as a subversive tool, not every legal move is the same in this respect. I still do not see how an extension of copyright privileges to street art can go on in an anti-establishment direction. Bringing street art *de jure* under the umbrella of copyright law is not a neutral act. Copyrightability comes at a cost, which in this case is both ontological and political. Understanding an artefact as subject to

224 Bey, 403.

225 Bey, 403. For a discussion of street art as a carnival, see also Baldini, "An Urban Carnival on the City Walls"; "Quand les murs de béton muets se transforment en un carnaval de couleur."

226 For a discussion of street art's relationship with authority, see also Baldini, "An Urban Carnival on the City Walls"; "Quand les murs de béton muets se transforment en un carnaval de couleur."

227 Dennis W. Allen, "Rtmark: Viral Activism and the Meaning of 'Post-Identity,'" *The Journal of the Midwest Modern Language Association* 36, no. 1 (2003): 6, https://doi.org/10.2307/1315395.

copyright inevitably pushes in favor of its commodification, that is, of conceptualizing it as a self-sufficient object that, among other things, can be bought and sold.[228] Such an ontological transition erodes street art's subversive potential. In other words, it goes against the nature of street art and its essential value.

The subversive power of street art is in effect primarily (though not exclusively) directed against the commodification of public space. This is particularly true in conventional contexts of creation of street art, that is, neo-liberal cities.[229] Street artworks subvert the commercial nature of urban spaces insofar as, among other things, they are *gifts* to the city. By following Michel de Certeau's influential account of public space, a gift is "transformed into a transgression in a profit economy: it appears as an excess (a waste), a challenge (a rejection of profit), or a crime (an attack on property)."[230] This subversive aspect of street art is stripped away when transformed into something copyrightable. Rather than preserving or promoting its anti-establishment nature, copyright tends to dilute and dissolve street art's subversiveness.

As a piece of evidence in favor of my reading of the risks of commodification embedded in appealing to copyright, one should observe how street artists' lawsuits against corporations for appropriating their works have been resolved: Settlements out of court have been the way to go.[231] In other words, the suing street artists and the sued companies have generally agreed on the payment of a fee for resolving their respective controversies. As these episodes suggest, copyright privileges seem to greatly encourage the commodification of street art: its buying and selling. By considering these legal cases and how they have been settled, the subversive argument does not seem to be a convincing answer to the justification question.

Before concluding this section, I want to make one point clear. I have no problems in accepting the claim that artists should be free to do whatever they want with their works: selling them, giving them away for free, destroying them, or trying to preserve them. In this sense, I am not going to give any

---

228 Martha Buskirk, "Commodification as Censor: Copyrights and Fair Use," *October* 60 (1992): 83–109, https://doi.org/10.2307/779036; Julie E. Cohen, "Copyright, Commodification, and Culture: Locating the Public Domain," SSRN Scholarly Paper (Rochester, NY: Social Science Research Network, 2005), https://papers.ssrn.com/abstract=663652; Fiona Macmillan, "Altering the Contours of the Public Domain," in *Intellectual Property: The Many Faces of the Public Domain*, ed. Charlotte Waelde and Hector L. MacQueen (Cheltenham, UK and Northampton, MA: Edward Elgar, 2007), 98–117.

229 For an analysis of street art and its value in unconventional street art contexts, see, for instance, Baldini and Pietrucci, "Knitting a Community Back Together."

230 de Certeau, *The Practice of Everyday Life*, 27. See also Irvine, "The Work on the Street," 252.

231 Finchett-Maddock, "In Vacuums of Law We Find," 10.

moralistic condemnation of the actions of REVOK or other street artists who have sued big corporations and accepting settlement fees. I am critical of certain ways of interpreting and justifying those lawsuits. Settling a lawsuit with a corporation for a fee simply is *not* an anti-establishment act, but rather a (legitimate) way to make a profit. At any rate, I believe it would be appropriate to agree that this has nothing to do with street art – at least as I intend it. Let us now turn to moral rights and their justification in street art.

## 5 *Against Moral Rights for Street Art*

Critically discussing artists' moral rights is a very unpopular approach: it is an academic 'taboo,' if I may say so. Whenever I have brought up my skepticism about the very existence of artists' moral rights at academic events, my doubts have been often received coldly, to put it mildly. In her perceptive analysis of current scholarship on moral rights, Amy Adler – one of the very few scholars who shares my doubts – offers a plausible explanation for such reactions to my heterodox views. In today's context, she has written, "if you don't support moral rights you're [seen as] a philistine who doesn't understand the sanctity of art."[232]

By considering the quasi-universal embracement of moral rights, I therefore expect that many will raise a suspicious eyebrow when reading these pages. Here, I am not interested in airing my concerns about moral rights in general. My aim here is to show the limits of this type of legislation regulating creativity within the context of street art. Of course, the present discussion points a finger at some controversial assumptions grounding moral rights. Moreover, part of street art's value is to help us critically engage with these doctrines.

Consider the right to attribution. It is unclear what should be a plausible justification for being concerned with legislation about reclaiming artistic paternity within the context of street art. Iljadica mentions at least three reasons showing why this moral right may very well be superfluous here.[233] First, many works of street art consist of the artist's signature.[234] This is of course the case in graffiti, where a writer's street name is usually the content of their work. Here, attribution, one might say, is embedded in the work itself. Second, if one accepts that street art is produced without the intention of being sold, there seems to be "no feasible advantage" in asserting one's name.[235] Third, works of street art are often realized by collectives such as *crews*, which do not

232 Amy Adler, "Against Moral Rights," *California Law Review* 97, no. 1 (2009): 264–65.

233 Iljadica, *Copyright Beyond Law*, chap. 8.

234 Iljadica, 218.

235 Iljadica, 219.

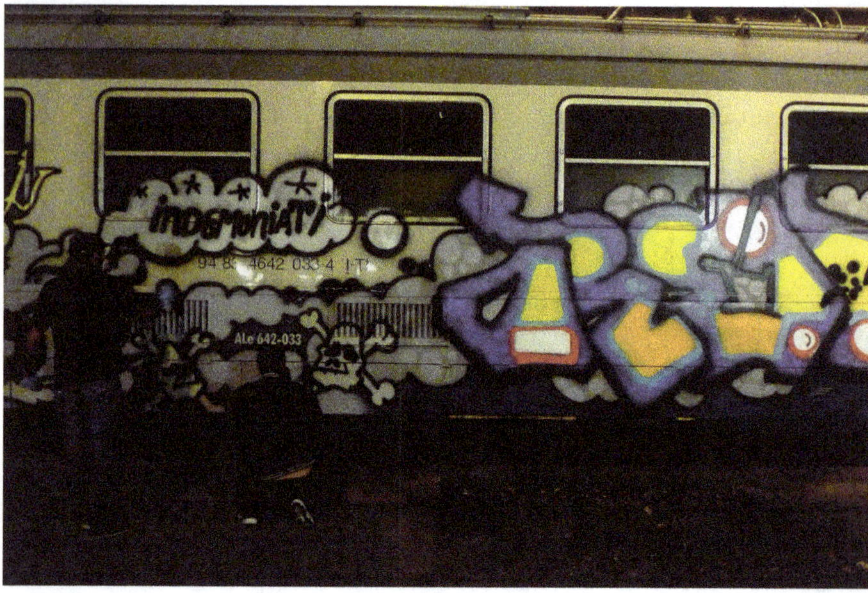


FIGURE 9 RSG crew in action
PHOTOGRAPH COURTESY OF FRA32

match the current parameters for joint attribution (fig. 9).[236] In these cases, it would be impossible for a crew to reclaim paternity of a particular piece, even if they wanted to. In many instances of genuine street art, then, concerns of attribution seem irrelevant.

By building on Iljadica's third idea, I would also press the point in ways that echo part of the previous section's discussion. The conceptual foundation of the right of attribution is grounded on a particular understanding of artistic authorship. In general, such a conception identifies a work's author with a particular individual or group of individuals. Street art has challenged this assumption perhaps more than any other modern art kinds, forms, or genres. It has blurred, challenged, and stretched our commonsensical conception of what an author is.

In their works on authorship, both Barthes and Foucault deconstruct the notion of authorship: In their respective views, identifying creators with individuals implies a series of assumptions that misrepresent how artistic practices function.[237] Such a distortion serves authoritarians ends insofar as it aims

236 Iljadica, 220.

237 Roland Barthes, "The Death of the Author," in *Image, Music, Text* (New York: Hill and Wang, 1977), 142–47; Michel Foucault, "What Is an Author?," in *Language, Counter-Memory,*

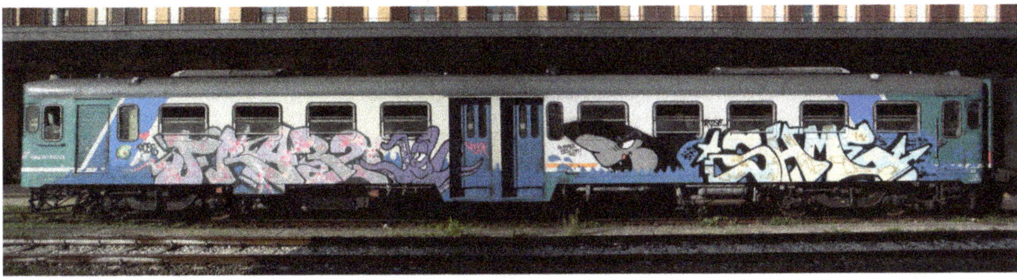

FIGURE 10 Fra32 and SAME exchanging names in Italy
PHOTOGRAPH COURTESY OF FRA32

at inhibiting a free circulation and exchange of creativity. Creative production is in this sense always a collective and dispersed activity, rather than the outcome of the actions of a god-like individual. What we have seen in recent developments of street art is the practical counterpart of Barthes's and Foucault's theoretical discussion.

With their recent works, the German duo MOSES and TAPS have radically called into question the idea of authorship to a point of its dissolution. They went beyond the use pseudonyms or anonymity, which is typical of street art. In INTERNATIONAL TOPSPRAYER™, the artists collected 1000 pieces done in 1000 days by an untold amount of people. "First MOSES and TAPS exchanged their names with each other, then they exchanged these names with friends from all over the world and finally they say that everybody can use "their" names – how could they even prevent it anyway?!"[238] By violating one of the unwritten rules of graffiti, MOSES and TAPS renounced their claim to their names and identities, thus making it impossible to connect individuals to examples of street art (fig. 10). Their work had such an impact on rights of attribution that it is cited in German courts to point out the discrepancy between names and identity. "Today," the duo adds, "the judges laugh when the prosecution explains their narrowminded story of a unique name as the most important thing in graffiti, and that nobody would ever copy it. A name is no longer proof." In the context of street art, rights of attribution as traditionally conceived with reference to mainstream art seem to do a poor job. To impose normative conceptions of authorship would thus introduce fatal

*Practice: Selected Essays and Interviews by Michel Foucault*, ed. Donald Bouchard (Ithaca, NY: Cornell University Press, 1977), 113–38.

238 Good Guy Boris, "MOSES AND TAPS™ – Exclusive Interview for The Grifters Journal," *The Grifters Journal* (blog), September 29, 2015, http://thegrifters.org/moses-and-taps-interview-exclusive-for-the-griters-journal/.

distortions into the nature and evolution of this urban creative practice. Street art is already beyond that. Once again, the current legal framework seems far from being a tool capable of protecting and promoting street art.

Let us now turn to the right of integrity. Moral justifications of extending legal restrictions of derogatory treatment and destruction of illegally installed pieces seem to be extremely problematic. The history of street art is essentially related to the buffing, whitewashing, crossing, and other destructive and derogatory phenomena. These are not accidental aspects of the practice. These are symptoms – and consequences – of its subversive nature and anarchic spirit. By echoing Banksy, if you want things to last, you should not paint them on a train car, wall, or whatever other interstice of the city landscape.[239] The erosion of street art's commitment to ephemerality may very well jeopardize the practice's essence by favoring, among other things, its commodification.

The possibility that one could interfere with the cultural dynamics of street art in fatal ways is a serious worry. Similarly to what I have said about copyright, it is not enough to rely on the idea that it is unlikely that street artists would appeal to moral rights in most cases. Legal frameworks open up and encourage new scenarios for actions. Furthermore, responses to recent legal cases, such as that of 5Pointz, that touch on questions of moral rights seem to be already encouraging and promoting certain dispositions to appeal to the law in cases possibly violating the right to integrity.[240]

I hasten to add that, in my view, what happened with 5Pointz bears little relevance for a discussion of street art and the right of integrity. In its latest stage, this famous cultural site only kept the appearance of what once was the hub of an incipient rebellious artistic movement that would have shook the world and started the trajectory of street art: writing. The site had lost all its subversiveness and had turned in what Pietro Rivasi has called, during our interview, "the death of graffiti."

As evidence in favor of my reading, consider the motivation that the court gave when recognizing the site's artistic stature, which was instrumental for recognizing the violation of artists' moral rights. As Bonadio writes, the relevance of 5Pointz was a function of having "become an attraction for

---

239 See CosmicdaisyUK, *Robbo vs Banksy – Graffiti Wars FULL VIDEO*, 2012, https://www.youtube.com/watch?v=ulOiB3xEkzM. The video reports the following comments by Banksy: "If you want things to last you shouldn't paint them under a bridge on the canal." This was a response to King Robbo. I discuss their feud in Baldini, "Beauty and the Behest."

240 See, for instance, Enrico Bonadio, "Preserving Street Art and Graffiti – Policy and Legal Issues," in *Copyright in Street Art and Graffiti – A Country-by-Country Legal Analysis*, ed. Enrico Bonadio (Cambridge: Cambridge University Press, forthcoming).

visitors to New York, with busloads of tourists, schoolchildren and even weddings heading to the site," a backdrop for movies, a presence in TV shows, and a prop for ad campaigns.[241] The judge also noted that artists who painted there showed "their professional achievements in terms of residences, teaching positions, fellowships, public and private commissions as well as media coverage and social media presence."[242] As Fra32 told me when discussing this sentence: "in graffiti, the street decides what's valuable, that is, the writers decide. It's not about the judge or the academics, who take into consideration commissions, artistic residencies, fellowships, and media coverage and presence. It's about getting up and style." I find in Fra32's analysis an expression of the true spirit of graffiti and – as I understand it – street art. 5Pointz is the opposite. Whatever happened, its fate in court is (and should) not be of much interest for the present discussion.

By considering my view about the relationship between street art and illegality, it should be obvious that I am *not* critical of 5Pointz because it is a legal spot. Halls of Fame and urban sites where painting is allowed have always existed and they are part of the culture(s) and the practice(s) of street art. They surely do not constitute the core of the practice, but they play an important role, and their neutral relationship with the law need not deprive them of subversiveness.

5Pointz is not a simple Hall of Fame, nor a mere spot where one can legally do graffiti. Its status reminds me of Leslie Hahner's and Scott Varda's interpretation of – at least some practices – of yarn bombing.[243] They claim that yarnbombing "is affirmed as a public good only inasmuch as it is the exceptional expression of the revolutionary potential of graffiti safeguarded through the provincial sensibilities of Western, middle class whiteness."[244] I see something similar at play with 5Pointz. There, we find aerosol art that appropriates the culture of graffiti and makes it palatable for white middleclass sensibility.

In effect – ironically, one might say – at the same time when many were appluading the ruling granting compensation to the 5Pointz artists, members

241 Enrico Bonadio, "How 21 Artists Graffitied One Man's Property, Made It Famous, Sued Him When He Knocked It down and Won $6.7m," *The Conversation*, February 17, 2018, http://theconversation.com/how-21-artists-graffitied-one-mans-property-made-it-famous-sued-him-when-he-knocked-it-down-and-won-6-7m-91933.

242 Bonadio.

243 Leslie A. Hahner and Scott J. Varda, "Yarn Bombing and the Aesthetics of Exceptionalism," *Communication and Critical/Cultural Studies* 11, no. 4 (2014): 301–21, https://doi.org/10.1080/14791420.2014.959453. Pamela Pietrucci and I have discussed cases of yarn bombing that do not fall under Hahner's and Varda's critical account. See Baldini and Pietrucci, "Knitting a Community Back Together."

244 Hahner and Varda, "Yarn Bombing and the Aesthetics of Exceptionalism," 302.

of the Spanish crew OTP were arrested three times and charged for graffiti vandalism.[245] Their arrest was made possible through a cooperation between NYPD and Interpol. Surprisingly enough, while on the one hand many were celebrating the inclusion of street art into the ivory tower of high art, writers were sent to jail. There is of course, a good dose of hypocrisy in all of this: the hypocrisy of accepting street art only when its revolutionary potential has been diluted and made palatable. In my view, 5Pointz is just that.

Before concluding this section, I should emphasize the following point: one could make an argument in favor of an extension of the right of integrity to street artworks in a specific case. Specifically, we would be inclined to extend this right in cases of unauthorized relocation. When cut from their original location and relocated in another location, perhaps a museum or a gallery, without the consent of the creator, street artworks seem to suffer in terms of their meaning and artistic value. For example, some of Blu's works were included in the exhibition *Banksy & Co.* without the artist's consent.[246] This curatorial choice has caused much controversy. Though my interest in rogue creativity finds something analogously seductive in rogue curatorial practices, I am open to considering the extension of this type of moral right to street art – at least to some extent.

## 6 *A New Paradigm of Copyright for Street Art*

In spite of my skepticism about the extension of copyright and moral rights to street art, I recognize that something should be done. Commercial appropriations of street artworks are becoming increasingly frequent. This is certainly a phenomenon that should be resisted and opposed. I agree with Bonadio on this respect: The use that big corporations make of street art is unjust and antithetical to the spirit of this urban creative practice. Contrary to his view, I do not consider copyright and moral rights as they stand now to be the appropriate move. What we need is a solution that balances the following

245 Elizabeth Rosner and Natalie O'Neill, "Accused Subway Vandal Arrested Again as He Leaves Court," *New York Post* (blog), April 23, 2018, https://nypost.com/2018/04/23/accused-subway-vandal-arrested-again-as-he-leaves-court/; Amanda Woods, Priscilla DeGregory, and Ruth Brown, "Interpol Helps NYPD Catch Subway Graffiti Artists," *New York Post* (blog), April 20, 2018, https://nypost.com/2018/04/20/interpol-helps-nypd-catch-subway-graffiti-artists/; Emily Saul, "Subway Vandals from Spain Avoid Jail for Graffiti Spree," *New York Post* (blog), June 14, 2018, https://nypost.com/2018/06/13/subway-vandals-from-spain-avoid-jail-for-graffiti-spree/.

246 Giovanni Vimercati, "Blu v Bologna: New Shades of Grey in the Street Art Debate," *The Guardian*, March 17, 2016, http://www.theguardian.com/artanddesign/2016/mar/17/street-artist-blu-destroys-murals-in-bologna.

twofold goals: protecting street art from commercial appropriation and keeping its subversiveness.[247]

The *pars construens* of my argument thus aims at being legally transformative; that is, it aims at promoting changes in the law that could serve the twofold goals just stated. This ambition distinguishes my view from those who are also critical of extending copyright to street art.[248] The good old days when commercial appropriation of street art was a marginal phenomenon are gone forever. The interest that this art kind generates naturally attracts attention from businesses and corporations. Ignoring this transformation allows for other forces antithetical to street art to play a key role in driving its evolution.[249]

Of course, my approach is philosophical. Therefore, I am not interested in discussing possible legal solutions from a technical point of view. Such discussions are beyond the scope of this project, and there are obviously scholars who are far better qualified to do that than me. My intention is to discuss what could possibly be the ethical foundation that should ground legislations dealing with the protection and promotion of street art. In other words, I am interested in framing the moral horizon wherein we should build our legal framework for protecting street art.

By drawing on recent scholarship on copynorms, I would like to suggest that legislation protecting street art should be built from the bottom up rather than from the top down. Attempts at connecting street art and copyright so far have tried to apply and adapt current laws and norms to the practice. What I propose is build a legislation from the ground-up: to start from the practice by finding participants' "understanding of social norms about the copying, distribution, and use of expressive works," which is the definition of

---

247 In an important sense, my proposal looks sympathetically at a piece of legislation dealing with the protection of street art that draws on cultural rights rather than intellectual property rights. Article 27 of the 1948 United Nations Declaration of Human Rights establishes, among other things, that all individuals have the right to participate in the cultural life of their communities, and to profit from cultural advancements (broadly construed). In this sense, cultural rights are group rights, and not just individual rights. I fully develop this theme in "Copyright Skepticism and Street Art: A Contrasting Opinion," in *Copyright in Street Art and Graffiti: A Country-by-Country Legal Analysis*, ed. Enrico Bonadio (Cambridge: Cambridge University Press, Forthcoming).

248 See, in particular, Merrill, "Keeping It Real?"; Finchett-Maddock, "In Vacuums of Law We Find."

249 My concern here echoes the main motive behind Pietro Rivasi's curatorial work on street art. With his exhibition *1984: Regeneration and Evolution of Writing*, Rivasi aims at guiding the inclusion of street art within institutional spaces in harmony with this art kind's grounding value. See Pietro Rivasi, *1984: Evoluzione e Rigenerazione Del Writing* (Modena: Galleria Civica di Modena, 2016).

copynorms.[250] The following step is to build a legal framework that can effectively accommodate those social norms without too much distortion.[251]

This strategy is analogous to what Creative Commons license (CC) tries to do. This license's goal is to provide a legal tool that "enables sharing and reuse of creativity and knowledge" by means of more flexible rules than those typical of traditional copyright.[252] Such rules revolve around CC's approach of "some rights reserved."[253] By promoting more relaxed ways to share the outcomes of one's creativity, "Creative Commons has succeeded in creating a new, alternative set of copynorms."[254] My hope is to encourage the creation of something similar explicitly dedicated to street art.

By looking at how, in the first place, practitioners and then appreciators of street art understand the copying, distributing, and using of street artworks, it seems reasonable to conceptualize examples of this urban art form as *public goods*.[255] The two following features characterize this variety of goods: (i) non-rivalry, and (ii) non-excludability. A public good *g* is non-rivalrous insofar as one person's enjoyment of *g* does not negatively affect other people's enjoyment of *g*. Moreover, *g* is not excludable when nobody can be prevented from enjoying *g*. Street artworks are non-rivalrous and non-excludable in the sense just specified.

As a consequence of their non-rivalrous and non-excludable nature, public goods cause market failures. In other words, this variety of good is generally unsuitable for generating profit. Therefore, no company would generally be interested in producing public goods. This aptly captures, in a technical sense,

---

250 Mark F. Schultz, "Copynorms: Copyright and Social Norms," SSRN Scholarly Paper (Rochester, NY: Social Science Research Network, 2006), 1, https://papers.ssrn.com/abstract=933656.

251 Here, I understand social norms as informal norms that individuals follow as a response to their expectations about other people's behaviors or beliefs. See Cristina Bicchieri, *The Grammar of Society: The Nature and Dynamics of Social Norms* (New York: Cambridge University Press, 2006); Cristina Bicchieri, *Norms in the Wild: How to Diagnose, Measure, and Change Social Norms* (New York: Oxford University Press, 2017).

252 "Frequently Asked Questions – Creative Commons," accessed August 2, 2018, https://creativecommons.org/faq/#what-is-creative-commons-and-what-do-you-do.

253 "Frequently Asked Questions – Creative Commons."

254 Schultz, "Copynorms," 19.

255 For an introductory discussion of public goods, see John Black, Nigar Hashimzade, and Gareth Myles, "Public Good," in *A Dictionary of Economics* (Oxford: Oxford University Press, 2017), http://www.oxfordreference.com/view/10.1093/acref/9780198759430.001.0001/acref-9780198759430-e-2513. See also Scott Barrett, *Why Cooperate? The Incentive to Supply Global Public Goods* (Oxford: Oxford University Press, 2007); Mancur Olson, *The Logic of Collective Action: Public Goods and the Theory of Groups* (Cambridge, MA; London: Harvard University Press, 1971).

the idea that street art is a gift to the city and how this in turn bears transgressive potential by violating the mechanisms of market economy in capitalist societies.

Legislation about copying, distributing, and using street art needs to account for the non-rivalry and non-excludability of street art. This in turn would also preserve and protect the exceptional economic nature of this artistic practice. In general, laws should prevent the commodification of street artworks – especially in the absence of artists' consent. Therefore, legislation should prevent the selling and buying of works spontaneously created by street artists using portions of the city landscape, even when the tangible medium belongs to someone who did not give their authorization for the creation of the work. (This point does not contradict some discussions about copyright and moral rights of street artists.)

Now that I have clarified the ideals that a legal framework regulating street art fair use should protect, let me venture to add a more specific proposal – or, better yet, a sketch of a proposal. In terms of uses (of reproductions) of the intangible work in commercial ads and campaigns, which I believe is the crucial test for every piece of legislation dealing with street art and copyright, I believe that we already have a legal framework that can offer an interesting starting point: the Copyright and Rights in Performances (Licensing of Orphan Works) Regulations 2014.[256]

The 2014 Regulations define orphan works as those works whose copyright holder is unknown or unreachable. When someone is interested in using an orphan work, these laws established a procedure by means of which the Intellectual Property Office may grant a non-exclusive license to do so. Here, we have a piece of legislation allowing persons to use a work that falls under copyright protection though under special circumstances, i.e., circumstances produced by a lack of knowledge of its author or whereabouts. It is worth mentioning that, rather than a subject, a dedicated commission is responsible for authorizing its use.

While disregarding the legal details of the 2014 Regulations, it seems to me that this piece of legislation opens up an interesting possibility for understanding and regulating copying, distribution, and use of street artworks. The legal horizon that it suggests is one where unauthorized cases of, among other things, the corporate appropriation of street art are handled by institutions rather than single artists. If suitably developed, a legal framework that is grounded on the decisions of a commission – especially if created from the

256 Bonadio mentions these laws in his discussion of anonymity in street art. See Bonadio, "Copyright Protection of Street Art and Graffiti under UK Law," 12.

ground up on the model of, for instance, Slow Food presidia – could more effectively serve the goal of fighting commercial appropriation without fostering commodification than current copyright norms.[257]

I see at least two advantages to this move. First, responses from a collective subject such as a commission treat the interest of all street artists fairly. It protects street art as a practice, and not only artists who are financially capable of lawyering up. It is not by chance that the only legal controversies of corporate appropriation of street art involved prominent street artists – and, in one case, the artist's estate. Those are, in general, the only subjects that can afford to deal with big companies and their legal advisors. However, street art is a holistic subcultural art kind whose life is essentially connected to the multiple local scenes. Protecting street art should also involve protecting its underground side, not only its superstars.

Here, one could also profit from new media technologies such as social media and other platforms of interaction that the web can offer as tool to create better strategies for testing the opinion of stakeholders. The use of social media like Instagram does not merely constitute the most common way to appreciate street art.[258] It is also an effective and privileged strategy for accessing "not only the field, but also the diversities and the peripheries of that field."[259] The protection of street art could greatly profit from the possibilities of new media technology.

Second, the impersonal control that a commission can exercise over licenses of use of street artworks is better suited to counteracting the risk of commodification. In other words, by working as a collective entity, a commission is – at least ideally – less likely to respond positively to proposals of out of court settlements for a fee. Since members of a commission overseeing authorizations of any kind are not allowed to personally receive compensation from the parties involved, one might hope that decisions could more closely follow the ideals and values that street art embodies as a practice.

At this point, one might say that the use of commissions for deciding on acceptable uses of street art from a legal standpoint is just another way of

257 For a description of Slow Food Presidia, see "Slow Food Presidia – What We Do," *Slow Food Foundation* (blog), accessed August 6, 2018, https://www.fondazioneslowfood.com/en/what-we-do/slow-food-presidia/.

258 Malcolm Jacobson, "The Dialectics of Graffiti Studies: A Personal Record of Documenting and Publishing on Graffiti since 1988," *Street Art and Urban Creativity Scientific Journal* 1, no. 2 (2015): 102.

259 Erik Hannerz, "Scrolling down the Line – a Few Notes on Using Instagram as Point of Access for Graffiti Research," *Street Art and Urban Creativity Scientific Journal* 2, no. 2 (2016): 37.

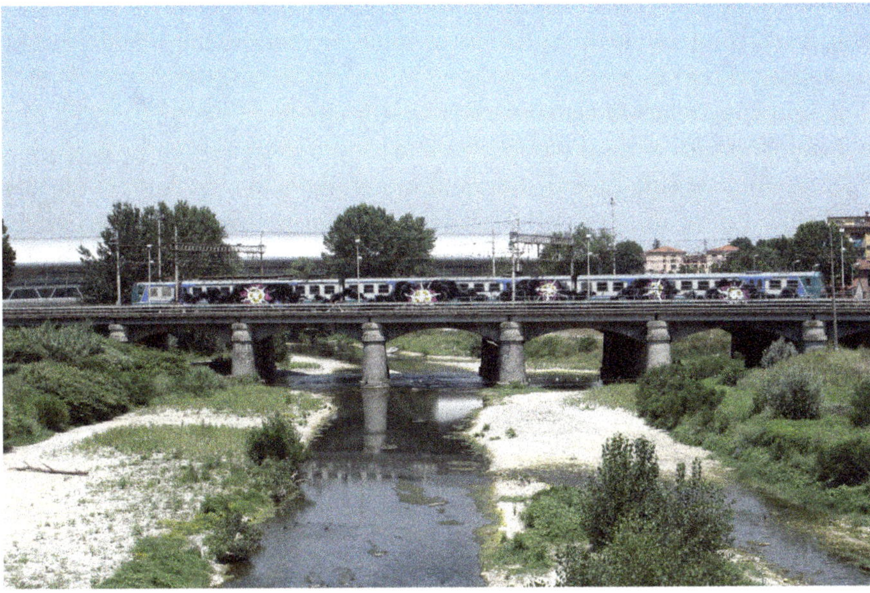

FIGURE 11 Zelle Asphaltkultur, *Detonation Boulevard #64* (ongoing project), 2016
PHOTO COURTESY OF THE ARTISTS. THE WORK WAS CREATED IN CONNECTION WITH RIVASI'S *1984*

institutionalizing street art. In this sense, one could add, it does not serve street art much better than current copyright laws. I do believe that there is something true to this objection. The creation of commissions for deciding fair use is an undeniable step in the direction of street art's institutionalization. Still, I do not believe that it is an evolution like anyone else. If suitably developed, it could help the transition of street art into this new phase.

In an important sense, this proposal echoes and follows in the footsteps of Rivasi's take on the musealization of street art. His curated exhibition of graffiti *1984* is exactly an attempt at institutionalizing street art by bringing it into the white cube while not eroding the practice's subversive potential. In this sense, Rivasi's brainchild successfully showed – I believe – "how to bring 'writing' into a museum respecting its spirit."[260] As Rivasi explicitly admits, *1984* was an attempt to cope with the desire of some street artists to engage with the artworld and possibly find recognition there without compromising the street art status of their work (fig. 11). In a similar sense, my proposal here wants to provide the foundation for a legal framework that could accommodate the

260 Rivasi, "Vandalism as Art: Unauthorized Paintings Vs Institutional Art Shows and Events – the Modena Case Study," 11.

desire of some street artists to engage with property rights while counteracting the risks of commodification and loss of subversiveness to the greatest extent possible.

Should copyright protect street art? In this chapter, I have addressed this question and furthermore interpreted a second order question by exploring whether an extension of copyright and moral rights to street art is ethically justifiable. I have raised a series of doubts about the possibility of finding such a justification. In general, current legislations of copyright and moral rights are inextricably intertwined with both exclusionary conceptions of creativity and tendencies to treat objects of art as mere commercial products. These implications in turn seriously challenge street art's essential subversiveness. Nonetheless, I have suggested a possible model for protecting street art from corporate appropriation, a model that is compatible – to the greatest extent that a proposal for a legal framework could be – with the anti-establishment nature of this urban art form. It might sound paradoxical, but perhaps the law could somehow play a role in preserving the subversiveness of street art.

## Conclusion: an Outlaw Art

Street art is one of the most interesting developments of the arts at the turn of the millennium – "and perhaps the most important of the last decades," as Joe Austin writes.[261] This urban art kind injected multiple novel developments in the world of Modern art. Surely, one of the crucial features that has made street art revolutionary from an artistic point of view, and also politically significant, is its use of vandalism as an artistic technique or tool. As I have discussed in this volume, street art has elevated breaking the law to more than just a crime by turning such a conflict into a feature that informs its existence as an artistic practice. In other words, its relationship with the law is a constitutive element of street art.

It would be incorrect to claim that street art is the only – or first – artistic genre to establish an intrinsic relationship with the law. "For the past century," as Maurizio Ferraris correctly points out, "conceptual art has, in fact, been contractual."[262] Contractual art, Ferraris explains, is art that has evolved in a direction "of essentially becoming a contract itself."[263] Artists involved in the

261 Austin, "More to See than a Canvas in a White Cube," 35.

262 Maurizio Ferraris, "Why Matter Matters," *Philosophical Readings* 2, no. 6 (2014): 6.

263 Ferraris, 6.

practice related to this art kind exploit legal loopholes to create artworks. This is the case, for instance, of Superflex's *Corruption Contract* (2009), where buyers commit themselves to extort or bribe. Another famous extreme example of contractual art is Robert Morris's *Document* (1963), a notarized text negating the aesthetic value of *Litanies*, another piece by Morris. In these works, "the bureaucratic frisson takes the place of other elements (information, emotion, aesthetic satisfaction) that were *constitutive* of traditional artworks."[264] In this sense, like street art, contractual art entertains an immanent relationship with the law.

The difference between how – respectively – street art and conceptual art relate to the law is found in the following point: If conceptual art is contractual art, street art is anti-contractual art. When I say that street art is anti-contractual, I mean that this urban art kind calls into question and rejects the assumptions that grounds the possibility of reducing artworks to contracts. Seen from the perspective of its relationship with the law, street art significantly challenges what Ferraris calls the "law of art," that is, "the canonical idea that an artwork is a physical thing, made by an author and endowed with an attractive appearance."[265] Against this background, street art is *outlaw art*.

As I have emphasized in discussing issues of copyright and moral rights in Chapter 3, street art embodies a variety of creativity that exceeds the canon of Western art. Its styles, techniques, and modes of creation, which rely on borrowing and appropriation, are often labeled as unoriginal, banal, and ugly – especially when considering the most radical examples of graffiti, that is, tags and throw-ups. Moreover, as we have seen exemplified in, for instance, MOSES and TAPS's INTERNATIONAL TOPSPRAYER™, street art also questions traditional conceptions of authorship, practically dissolving the substantive notions of the author that Barthes and Foucault theoretically deconstructed in their respective works. My skepticism about the extension of copyright and moral rights to street art comes exactly from the potential distortions that laws envisioned to promote and protect mainstream Western artistic practices would necessarily introduce into the practice. More specifically, what I fear is the risk of commodification that intellectual property laws carry within themselves. Commodification is central to contractual art and is the antithesis of anti-contractual art, which cannot be reduced to a good for exchange.

Insofar as it is outlaw art, street art also provides us with an alternative way to conceptualize the relationship between art and vandalism. As I have

264 Ferraris, 8.

265 Ferraris, 6.

discussed in Chapter 2, the exclusive disjunction separating art from vandalism that seems so popular among commentators and discussants of street art, both inside and outside academia, is a conceptual non-starter. There seems to be no plausible way to construe such an exclusive disjunction. Nothing seems to prevent particulars from being both art and vandalism. In the case of street artworks, something more is also at play. Street artworks are not mere examples of art and vandalism. More interestingly, their vandalism significantly influences the creation of their meaning as objects of art, that is, in the conferral of their artistic status. In this sense, I have suggested that street art is art (partly) because of its vandalism.

Street art's illegality – primarily its vandalism – is, though, not a feature whose presence is essential for something to be a genuine example of street art. Street art need not be illegal. As I have argued in Chapter 1, being illegal is neither a necessary nor a sufficient condition of street art. 'Being illegal,' in effect, is a distinctly legal notion that is formally specified within legal systems. What is illegal, in other words, is clearly determined by the decisions of judges or other specialized legal appointees. If street art were necessarily illegal, judges would have to be the ultimate *arbiter elegantiae* of street art thanks to their authority of deciding what is and is not street art. But this is obviously a reduction to absurdity. Moreover, I have also shown that there are clear cases of illegal commercial art that do not qualify as street art for their lack of subversiveness.

Illegality, I have argued, in effect, is a crucial tactic by means of which street artists imbue their works with subversive value. Such value identifies the essence of this urban artistic practice as the artistic practice that it is. Street art's subversiveness is a function of its capacity to challenge dominant uses of public spaces. The unauthorized and unsanctioned appropriation of public and private property is key to unleashing this potential. The recurrent and salient illegal nature of examples of street art functions as a ground for street art's subversiveness, injecting the practice as a whole with a rebellious charge that also legal examples share in virtue of their connection with the most confrontational aspects of the practice. If it is true that street art need not be illegal, it is also the case that street art cannot be completely legalized: it would normalize it and turn it into a form of mainstream art.

One need not romanticize the outlaw nature of street art. Its anarchic spirit introduces destructive elements into the life of our cities: It unilaterally imposes – albeit momentarily – certain aesthetic conceptions of the urban landscape on virtually all residents. If for some street art imbues the grey cement of our walls with colors and intriguing forms, for others, one must accept it, it brings damage and destruction to the streets. However, politically, its message is liberating and potentially enriching.

By unapologetically imposing its alternative conception of the aesthetics of urban spaces, street art denounces the authoritarianism of dominant spatial politics, which favor only certain forms of expression and communication, while violently opposing others. In particular, dominant policies ferociously oppose and outlaw those forms of expression that exceed the logic of the profit that has come to dominate the life of the city, whose streets and squares are almost completely commodified. Street art shows that there are alternative ways to use space, ways that are freer, more creative, and possibly non-exclusionary. But, indeed, market forces are powerful, and it is unclear whether street art will be domesticated and turned into a hot commodity – a transformation that in part is already at play. This work has been, overall, an attempt to identify these unfortunate transformations and to counteract them, in light of the positive changes that street art can bring to our urban lives. Street art is fighting the law. As for who will win, that we cannot know.

## References

Abarca, Javier. "From Street Art to Murals: What Have We Lost?" *Street Art and Urban Creativity Scientific Journal* 2, no. 2 (2016): 60–67.

Adler, Amy. "Against Moral Rights." *California Law Review* 97, no. 1 (2009): 263–300.

Allen, Dennis W. "Rtmark: Viral Activism and the Meaning of 'Post-Identity.'" *The Journal of the Midwest Modern Language Association* 36, no. 1 (2003): 6–24. https://doi.org/10.2307/1315395.

Andina, Tiziana. *The Philosophy of Art: The Question of Definition: From Hegel to Post-Dantian Theories*. London: Bloomsbury Academic, 2013.

Andina, Tiziana. *What Is Art?: The Question of Definition Reloaded*. Leiden: Brill, 2017.

Anenson, T. Leigh. "Limiting Legal Remedies: An Analysis of Unclean Hands." *Kentucky Law Journal* 99 (2011): 63–118.

"Another Graffiti Copyright Claim against a Major Brand – Robbins v Oakley." Accessed June 25, 2018. http://uspatentlaw.cn/en/another-graffiti-copyright-claim-against-a-major-brand-robbins-v-oakley/.

Austin, Joe. "More to See than a Canvas in a White Cube: For an Art in the Streets." *City* 14, no. 1–2 (2010): 33–47. https://doi.org/10.1080/13604810903529142.

Austin, Joe. *Taking the Train: How Graffiti Art Became an Urban Crisis in New York City*. New York and Chichester, UK: Columbia University Press, 2001.

Bacharach, Sondra. "Finding Your Voice in the Streets: Street Art and Epistemic Injustice." *The Monist* 101, no. 1 (2018): 31–43. https://doi.org/10.1093/monist/onx033.

Bacharach, Sondra. "Street Art and Consent." *The British Journal of Aesthetics* 55, no. 4 (2015): 481–95. https://doi.org/10.1093/aesthj/ayv030.

Baker, Laura E. "Public Sites versus Public Sights: The Progressive Response to Outdoor Advertising and the Commercialization of Public Space." *American Quarterly* 59, no. 4 (2007): 1187–1213.

Baldini, Andrea. "An Urban Carnival on the City Walls: The Visual Representation of Financial Power in European Street Art." *Journal of Visual Culture* 14, no. 2 (2015): 246–52. https://doi.org/10.1177/1470412915592883.

Baldini, Andrea. "Beauty and the Behest: Distinguishing Legal Judgment and Aesthetic Judgment in the Context of 21st Century Street Art and Graffiti." *Rivista Di Estetica* 65 (2017): 91–106. https://doi.org/10.4000/estetica.2161.

Baldini, Andrea. "Copyright Skepticism and Street Art: A Contrasting Opinion." In *Copyright in Street Art and Graffiti: A Country-by-Country Legal Analysis*, edited by Enrico Bonadio. Cambridge: Cambridge University Press, Forthcoming.

Baldini, Andrea. "Dangerous Liaisons: Graffiti in Da Museum." In *Un(Authorized)// Commissioned*, by Pietro Rivasi and Andrea Baldini, 26–32. Rome: WholeTrain Press, 2018.

Baldini, Andrea. "Public Art: A Critical Approach." Temple University Libraries, 2014.

Baldini, Andrea. "Quand les murs de béton muets se transforment en un carnaval de couleur. Le street art comme stratégie de résistance sociale contre le modèle commercial de la visibilité." *Cahiers de Narratologie. Analyse et Théorie Narratives* 30 (2016).

Baldini, Andrea. "Street Art: A Reply to Riggle." *The Journal of Aesthetics and Art Criticism* 74, no. 2 (2016): 187–91.

Baldini, Andrea, and Pamela Pietrucci. "Knitting a Community Back Together: Spontaneous Public Art as Citizenship Engagement in Post-Earthquake L'Aquila." In *Territories of Political Participation. Public Art, Urban Design, and Performative Citizenship*, edited by Luigi Musarò and Laura Iannelli, 115–32. Milan: Mimesis International, 2017.

Banksy. *Wall and Piece*. London: Century, 2005.

Barnes, Bradley R., Noel Y. M. Siu, Qionglei Yu, and Sally S. Y. Chan. "Exploring Cosmetics Advertising in Southern China." *International Journal of Advertising* 28, no. 2 (2009): 369–93. https://doi.org/10.2501/S0265048709200606.

Barrett, Scott. *Why Cooperate? The Incentive to Supply Global Public Goods*. Oxford: Oxford University Press, 2007.

Barthes, Roland. "The Death of the Author." In *Image, Music, Text*, 142–47. New York: Hill and Wang, 1977.

Bengtsen, Peter. "Carelessness or Curatorial Chutzpah? On Controversies Surrounding Street Art in the Museum." *Konsthistorisk Tidskrift/Journal of Art History* 84, no. 4 (2015): 220–33. https://doi.org/10.1080/00233609.2015.1095797.

Bernhard, Michael. "The Polish Opposition and the Technology of Resistance," n.d. http://www.clas.ufl.edu/users/bernhard/content/Solid3.pdf.

Besser, Jens. "Cash for Chaos. Marketing, Self-Support, Bonds and Funding and in the Field of Trainpainting." In *1984: Evoluzione e Rigenerazione Del Writing*, edited by Pietro Rivasi, 26–27. Modena: Galleria Civica di Modena, 2016.

Bey, Hakim. *T.A.Z: The Temporary Autonomous Zone, Ontological Anarchy, Poetic Terrorism*. Boulder, CO: Wiretap; NetLibrary, 1991.

Bey, Hakim. "The Temporary Autonomous Zone." In *Crypto Anarchy, Cyberstates, and Pirate Utopias*, edited by Peter Ludlow, 401–34. Cambridge, MA and London, UK: MIT Press, 2001.

Bicchieri, Cristina. *Norms in the Wild: How to Diagnose, Measure, and Change Social Norms*. New York: Oxford University Press, 2017.

Bicchieri, Cristina. *The Grammar of Society: The Nature and Dynamics of Social Norms*. New York: Cambridge University Press, 2006.

Biederman, Susan Duke, ed. "Symposium on Law and the Visual Arts." *Nova Law Review* 14, no. 2 (1990): 305–582.

Birney, Adrian. "Crack Puns: Text and Context in an Item of Latrinalia." *Western Folklore* 32, no. 2 (1973): 137–40. https://doi.org/10.2307/1498326.

Black, John, Nigar Hashimzade, and Gareth Myles. "Public Good." In *A Dictionary of Economics*. Oxford: Oxford University Press, 2017. http://www.oxfordreference.com/view/10.1093/acref/9780198759430.001.0001/acref-9780198759430-e-2513.

Blanché, Ulrich. "Qu'est-ce que le Street art? Essai et discussion des définitions." *Cahiers de Narratologie. Analyse et théorie narratives*, no. 29 (2015). https://doi.org/10.4000/narratologie.7397.

Blanché, Ulrich. "Street Art and Related Terms – Discussion and Working Definition." *Street Art and Urban Creativity Scientific Journal* 1 (2015): 32–39.

Boden, Margaret A. *Creativity and Art: Three Roads to Surprise*. Oxford: Oxford University Press, 2010.

Bonadio, Enrico. "Copyright Protection of Street Art and Graffiti under UK Law." SSRN Scholarly Paper. Rochester, NY: Social Science Research Network, 2017. https://papers.ssrn.com/abstract=2946360.

Bonadio, Enrico. "How 21 Artists Graffitied One Man's Property, Made It Famous, Sued Him When He Knocked It down and Won $6.7m." *The Conversation*, February 17, 2018. http://theconversation.com/how-21-artists-graffitied-one-mans-property-made-it-famous-sued-him-when-he-knocked-it-down-and-won-6-7m-91933.

Bonadio, Enrico. "Preserving Street Art and Graffiti – Policy and Legal Issues." In *Copyright in Street Art and Graffiti – A Country-by-Country Legal Analysis*, edited by Enrico Bonadio. Cambridge: Cambridge University Press, Forthcoming.

Borghini, Andrea. "What Is a Recipe?" *Journal of Agricultural and Environmental Ethics* 28, no. 4 (2015): 719–38.

Boris, Good Guy. "MOSES AND TAPS™ – Exclusive Interview for The Grifters Journal." *The Grifters Journal* (blog), September 29, 2015. http://thegrifters.org/moses-and-taps-interview-exclusive-for-the-griters-journal/.

Brighenti, Andrea. "At the Wall: Graffiti Writers, Urban Territoriality, and the Public Domain." *Space and Culture* 13, no. 3 (2010): 315–32. https://doi.org/10.1177/1206331210365283.

Brighenti, Andrea. "Graffiti, Street Art and the Divergent Synthesis of Place Valorisation in Contemporary Urbanism." In *Routledge Handbook of Graffiti and Street Art*, edited by Jeffrey Ian Ross, 158–67. New York: Routledge, 2016.

Brown, Evan. "Fixed Perspectives: The Evolving Contours of the Fixation Requirement in Copyright Law." *Washington Journal of Law, Technology & Arts* 10 (2014): 17–34.

Buffenstein, Alyssa. "Did McDonald's Steal Dash Snow's Grafitti Tag?" *artnet News*, October 5, 2016. https://news.artnet.com/art-world/dash-snows-family-sues-mcdonalds-copyright-infringement-685901.

Buskirk, Martha. "Commodification as Censor: Copyrights and Fair Use." *October* 60 (1992): 83–109. https://doi.org/10.2307/779036.

Campos, Ricardo. "Graffiti Writer as Superhero." *European Journal of Cultural Studies* 16, no. 2 (2013): 155–70. https://doi.org/10.1177/1367549412467177.

Carroll, Noël. "Art, Intention, and Conversation." In *Intention and Interpretation*, edited by Gary Iseminger, 97–131. Philadelphia, PA: Temple University Press, 1992.

"Caso di Alice Pasquini, street artist conosciuta come AliCè." Accessed June 10, 2018. http://www.associazioneantigraffiti.it/2016/02/21/caso-di-alice-pasquini-street-artist-conosciuta-come-alice/.

Certeau, Michel de. *The Practice of Everyday Life*. Berkeley and Los Angeles, CA: University of California Press, 1984.

Certeau, Michel de, and Luce Giard. *Culture in the Plural*. Minneapolis: University of Minnesota Press, 1998.

Chackal, Tony. "Of Materiality and Meaning: The Illegality Condition in Street Art." *The Journal of Aesthetics and Art Criticism* 74, no. 4 (2016): 359–70. https://doi.org/10.1111/jaac.12325.

Cohen, Julie E. "Copyright, Commodification, and Culture: Locating the Public Domain." SSRN Scholarly Paper. Rochester, NY: Social Science Research Network, 2005. https://papers.ssrn.com/abstract=663652.

Confino, Jo. "'Fake Street Art Sucks': Perrier Replaces Williamsburg's Nelson Mandela Mural." *The Guardian*, September 26, 2014, sec. Guardian Sustainable Business. http://www.theguardian.com/sustainable-business/2014/sep/26/fake-street-art-sucks-perrier-replaces-williamsburgs-nelson-mandela-mural-with-huge-advertisement.

CosmicdaisyUK. *Robbo vs Banksy – Graffiti Wars FULL VIDEO*, 2012. https://www.youtube.com/watch?v=ulOiB3xEkzM.

Creative Foundation v Dreamland Leisure Ltd [2015] EWHC 2556 (Ch) (September 11, 2015).

Damich, Edward J. "A Critique of the Visual Artists Rights Act of 1989." *Nova Law Review* 14, no. 2 (1990): 407–20.

Danto, Arthur C. *The Transfiguration of the Commonplace: A Philosophy of Art*. Cambridge, MA: Harvard University Press, 1981.

Danto, Arthur C. "The Artworld." *The Journal of Philosophy* 61 (1964): 571–84.

Danto, Arthur C. "Tilted Arc and Public Art." In *The State of the Art*. New York, NY: Prentice-Hall Press, 1987.

Danysz, Magda. *From Style Writing to Art: A Street Art Anthology*. Rome: DRAGO, 2010.

"Dash Snow." *Artnet* (blog). Accessed July 1, 2018. http://www.artnet.com/artists/dash-snow/.

Davies, David. *Art as Performance*. Malden, MA and Oxford, UK: Blackwell, 2004.

Dewey, John. *Art as Experience*. New York: Perigee Books, 1980.

Douzinas, Costas, Shaun McVeigh, and Ronnie Warrington. "The Alta(e)Rs of Law: The Judgement of Legal Aesthetics." *Theory, Culture & Society* 9, no. 4 (1992): 93–117. https://doi.org/10.1177/026327692009004005.

Dundes, Alan. *Meaning of Folklore: The Analytical Essays of Alan Dundes*. Logan: Utah State University Press, 2007.

Dworkin, Ronald. *Law's Empire*. Cambridge, MA: Belknap Press, 1986.

"Exclusive Interview with Utah & Ether, Graffiti's Bonnie & Clyde." *The Hundreds*. Accessed May 11, 2017. https://thehundreds.com/blogs/content/utah-ether-interview.

"EXCLUSIVE: Speaking to … OKER." *Wavey Garms*. Accessed May 10, 2018. https://waveygarms.com/blogs/news/speaking-to-oker.

Feist Publications, Inc., v. Rural Telephone Service Co., No. 499 U.S. 340 (1991).

Ferraris, Maurizio. "Why Matter Matters." *Philosophical Readings* 2, no. 6 (2014): 4–25.

Ferrell, Jeff. *Crimes of Style. Urban Graffiti and the Politics of Criminality*. Boston, MA: Northeastern University Press, 1996.

Feuer, Alan. "Brooklyn Lawsuit Asks If Illegal Graffiti Is Protected by Copyright Law." *The New York Times*, March 15, 2018, sec. New York. https://www.nytimes.com/2018/03/15/nyregion/brooklyn-graffiti-hm-lawsuit.html.

Feuer, Alan. "Graffiti Artists Awarded $6.7 Million for Destroyed 5Pointz Murals." *The New York Times*, February 13, 2018, sec. New York. https://www.nytimes.com/2018/02/12/nyregion/5pointz-graffiti-judgment.html.

Finchett-Maddock, Lucy. "In Vacuums of Law We Find: Outsider Poiesis in Street Art and Graffiti." SSRN Scholarly Paper. Rochester, NY: Social Science Research Network, 2017. https://papers.ssrn.com/abstract=3066309.

Fischer, Benjamin B. "Solidarity, the CIA, and Western Technology." *International Journal of Intelligence and CounterIntelligence* 25, no. 3 (2012): 427–69. https://doi.org/10.1080/08850607.2012.652523.

Fodor, Jerry A., and Ernest LePore. *Holism: A Shopper's Guide*. Oxford, UK and Cambridge, MA: Blackwell, 1992.

Foucault, Michel. *Discipline and Punish: The Birth of the Prison*. New York: Vintage Books, 1995.

Foucault, Michel. "Practicing Criticism." In *Michel Foucault: Politics Philosophy, Culture Interviews and Other Writings 1977–1984*, edited by L. D. Kritzman, 152–156. New York: Routledge, 1988.

Foucault, Michel. "What Is an Author?" In *Language, Counter-Memory, Practice: Selected Essays and Interviews by Michel Foucault*, edited by Donald Bouchard, translated by Donald Bouchard and Sherry Simon, 113–38. Ithaca, NY: Cornell University Press, 1977.

"Frequently Asked Questions – Creative Commons." Accessed August 2, 2018. https://creativecommons.org/faq/#what-is-creative-commons-and-what-do-you-do.

Geertz, Clifford. "Deep Hanging Out." *The New York Review of Books* 45, no. 16 (October 22, 1998): 69–72.

Girolamo, Domenico De, and Andrew Dale. *Glorious Attitude / Fra32*. Rome: Whole Train Press, 2018.

Goede, Marieke de. "Carnival of Money. Politics of Dissent in an Era of Globalizing Finance." In *The Global Resistance Reader*, edited by Louise Amoore, 379–391. London and New York: Routledge, 2005.

Gomez, Marisa A. "The Writing on Our Walls: Finding Solutions through Distinguishing Graffiti Art from Graffiti Vandalism." *University of Michigan Journal of Law Reform* 26 (1993): 633–708.

"Graffiti Artists Sue Cavalli." *Widewalls*. Accessed May 1, 2018. https://www.widewalls.ch/graffiti-artists-sue-cavalli.

Griffin, Jamie. "Illegal Graffiti: A Copyright Perspective." *Intellectual Property Law Bulletin* 20 (2010): 123–55.

Hahner, Leslie A., and Scott J. Varda. "Yarn Bombing and the Aesthetics of Exceptionalism." *Communication and Critical/Cultural Studies* 11, no. 4 (2014): 301–21. https://doi.org/10.1080/14791420.2014.959453.

Hannerz, Erik. *Performing Punk*. New York, NY: Palgrave Macmillan, 2015.

Hannerz, Erik. "Scrolling down the Line – a Few Notes on Using Instagram as Point of Access for Graffiti Research." *Street Art and Urban Creativity Scientific Journal* 2, no. 2 (2016): 37–41.

"H&M VS Jason Revok Williams and the Problem of Street Art." *nss magazine*. Accessed July 27, 2018. https://www.nssmag.com/en/article/14226.

Horowitz, Gregg M. "Public Art/Public Space: The Spectacle of the Tilted Arc Controversy." *The Journal of Aesthetics and Art Criticism* 54, no. 1 (1996): 8–14.

Humphreys, Paul. *Emergence*. Oxford: Oxford University Press, 2016.

Humphreys, Paul. "Emergence, Not Supervenience." *Philosophy of Science* 64, no. 4 (1997): S337 S345.

Hunter, Garry. *Street Art: From Around the World*. London: Arcturus Publishing, 2013.

Iljadica, Marta. *Copyright Beyond Law: Regulating Creativity in the Graffiti Subculture*. London: Bloomsbury Publishing, 2016.

Iljadica, Marta. "Graffiti and the Moral Right of Integrity." *Intellectual Property Quarterly* 3 (2015): 266–88.

Iljadica, Marta. "Street Art Belongs to the Freeholder." *Journal of Intellectual Property Law & Practice* 11, no. 2 (2016): 90–91. https://doi.org/10.1093/jiplp/jpv230.

"Invader – About." Accessed February 7, 2016. http://www.space-invaders.com/about/.

Irvine, Martin. "The Work on the Street: Street Art and Visual Culture." In *The Handbook of Visual Culture*, edited by Ian Heywood, Barry Sandywell, Michael Gardiner, Gunalan Nadarajan, and Catherine M. Soussloff, 235–78. London: Berg, 2012.

Iveson, Kurt. "Branded Cities: Outdoor Advertising, Urban Governance, and the Outdoor Media Landscape." *Antipode* 44, no. 1 (2012): 151–74. https://doi.org/10.1111/j.1467-8330.2011.00849.x.

Iveson, Kurt. "Cities within the City: Do-It-Yourself Urbanism and the Right to the City." *International Journal of Urban and Regional Research* 37, no. 3 (2013): 941–56. https://doi.org/10.1111/1468-2427.12053.

Iveson, Kurt. *Publics and the City*. Malden, MA and Oxford, UK: Blackwell Publishing, 2007.

Iveson, Kurt. "The Wars on Graffiti and the New Military Urbanism." *City* 14, no. 1–2 (2010): 115–34. https://doi.org/10.1080/13604810903545783.

Jacobson, Malcolm. "The Dialectics of Graffiti Studies: A Personal Record of Documenting and Publishing on Graffiti since 1988." *Street Art and Urban Creativity Scientific Journal* 1, no. 2 (2015): 99–103.

Jones, Amelia. *Body Art/Performing the Subject*. Minneapolis; London: University of Minnesota Press, 1998.

Keating, Gregory C. "Justifying Hercules: Ronald Dworkin and the Rule of Law." *American Bar Foundation Research Journal* 1987 (1987): 525–38.

Keith, Michael. *After the Cosmopolitan? Multicultural Cities and the Future of Racism*. London; New York: Routledge, 2005.

Kennedy, Maev. "Banksy Stencil Soars Past Hay Wain as UK's Favourite Work of Art." *The Guardian*, July 25, 2017. https://www.theguardian.com/artanddesign/2017/jul/26/banksy-balloon-girl-hay-wain-favourite-uk-work-of-art-constable-poll-nation.

Kilcooley-O'Halloran, Scarlett. "Cavalli's Graffiti War Wages On." *British Vogue*. Accessed May 1, 2018. http://www.vogue.co.uk/article/graffiti-artists-respond-roberto-cavalli-lawsuit.

Kindynis, Theo. "Bomb Alert: Graffiti Writing and Urban Space in London." *The British Journal of Criminology* 58, no. 3 (2018). https://doi.org/doi:10.1093/bjc/azx040.

Knight, Cher Krause. *Public Art: Theory, Practice and Populism*. Malden, MA: Blackwell, 2008.

Kwon, Miwon. *One Place After Another: Site-Specific Art and Locational Identity*. Cambridge, MA: MIT Press, 2004.

Lamarque, Peter. *The Philosophy of Literature*. Malden, MA: Blackwell, 2009.

*Le reazioni dei napoletani alla pizza all'ananas*. Accessed May 6, 2018. https://youmedia.fanpage.it/video/ab/WfNoxOSwgwL3Hnux.

Lessig, Lawrence. *The Future of Ideas: The Fate of the Commons in a Connected World*. New York: Random House, 2001.

Lijster, Thijs, Steven C. Dubin, Mark Antliff, and James Miller. "Politics." In *Encyclopedia of Aesthetics*, edited by Michael Kelly, 2nd ed. Oxford: Oxford University Press, 2014. http://www.oxfordreference.com/view/10.1093/acref/9780199747108.001.0001/acref-9780199747108-e-575.

Lopes, Dominic McIver. *A Philosophy of Computer Art*. New York: Routledge, 2009.

Lopes, Dominic McIver. "Aesthetic Experts, Guides to Value." *The Journal of Aesthetics and Art Criticism* 73, no. 3 (2015): 235–46. https://doi.org/10.1111/jaac.12170.

Lopes, Dominic McIver. *Beyond Art*. Oxford: Oxford University Press, 2014.

Lopes, Dominic McIver. "The Myth of (Non-Aesthetic) Artistic Value." *The Philosophical Quarterly* 61, no. 244 (2011): 518–36. https://doi.org/10.1111/j.1467-9213.2011.700.x.

Lopez-Pumarejo, Tomas A., and Myles Bassell. "The Renaissance of Outdoor Advertising: From Harlem to Hong Kong." *American Journal of Business* 24, no. 2 (2009): 33–40. https://doi.org/10.1108/19355181200900009.

Macmillan, Fiona. "Altering the Contours of the Public Domain." In *Intellectual Property: The Many Faces of the Public Domain*, edited by Charlotte Waelde and Hector L. MacQueen, 98–117. Cheltenham, UK and Northampton, MA: Edward Elgar, 2007.

Margolis, Joseph. *Moral Philosophy After 9/11*. University Park, PA: Pennsylvania State University Press, 2004.

Margolis, Joseph. "The Importance of Being Earnest about the Definition and Metaphysics of Art." *The Journal of Aesthetics and Art Criticism* 68, no. 3 (2010): 215–23. https://doi.org/10.1111/j.1540-6245.2010.01413.x.

Margolis, Joseph. *What, After All, Is a Work of Art?: Lectures in the Philosophy of Art*. University Park, PA: Pennsylvania State University Press, 1999.

Martin, Elizabeth, and Jonathan Law "Criminal Damage." *A Dictionary of Law*. Oxford: Oxford University Press, 2015.

Martin, Elizabeth, and Jonathan Law. "Vandalism." *A Dictionary of Law*. Oxford: Oxford University Press, 2015.

Mattelart, Armand. *Advertising International: The Privatization of Public Space*. London and New York: Routledge, 1991.

McAuliffe, Cameron, and Kurt Iveson. "Art and Crime (and Other Things Besides …): Conceptualising Graffiti in the City." *Geography Compass* 5, no. 3 (2011): 128–43. https://doi.org/10.1111/j.1749-8198.2011.00414.x.

Merrill, Samuel. "Keeping It Real? Subcultural Graffiti, Street Art, Heritage and Authenticity." *International Journal of Heritage Studies* 21, no. 4 (2015): 369–89. https://doi.org/10.1080/13527258.2014.934902.

Meskin, Aaron. "Style." In *Routledge Companion to Aesthetics*, edited by Berys Gaut and Dominic McIver Lopes, 3rd ed., 442–51. London: Routledge, 2013.

Metix (UK) Ltd v G H Maughan (Plastics) Ltd, No. FSR 718 (1997).

Mettler, Margaret L. "Graffiti Museum: A First Amendment Argument for Protecting Uncommissioned Art on Private Property." *Michigan Law Review* 111, no. 2 (2012): 249–81.

Mitzman, Dany. "The Day I Ordered Pizza That 'Doesn't Exist.'" *BBC News*, August 5, 2015, sec. Magazine. https://www.bbc.com/news/magazine-33542392.

Mothersill, Mary. "Aesthetic Laws, Principles and Properties: A Response to Eddy Zemach." *The Journal of Aesthetics and Art Criticism* 47, no. 1 (1989): 77–82. https://doi.org/10.2307/431995.

Mothersill, Mary. "Aesthetics: The Need for a Theory." *Midwest Studies In Philosophy* 24, no. 1 (2000): 244–54. https://doi.org/10.1111/1475-4975.00033.

Mothersill, Mary. *Beauty Restored*. Oxford, UK: Clarendon Press, 1984.

"Oakley Claims Artists' Graffiti Is Too 'Generic' to Be Copyrighted." *Artsy*, June 14, 2018. https://www.artsy.net/news/artsy-editorial-two-graffiti-artists-sued-oakley-clothing-brand-work-ads-permission.

"Oakley Denies Validity of Graffiti Copyright." *HYPEBEAST*. Accessed June 25, 2018. https://hypebeast.com/2018/6/oakley-denies-validity-of-graffiti-copyright.

O'Connor, Timothy, and Hong Yu Wong. "Emergent Properties." In *The Stanford Encyclopedia of Philosophy*, edited by Edward N. Zalta. Summer 2015. https://plato.stanford.edu/archives/sum2015/entries/properties-emergent/.

O'Hear, Anthony. "Art and Censorship." *Philosophy* 66, no. 258 (1991): 512–16.

Olson, Mancur. *The Logic of Collective Action: Public Goods and the Theory of Groups*. Cambridge, MA; London: Harvard University Press, 1971.

Pan, Lu. "Writing at the End of History: Reflections on Two Cases of Graffiti in Hong Kong." *Public Art Dialogue* 4, no. 1 (2014): 147–66. https://doi.org/10.1080/21502552.2014.878487.

Pfaelzar, Jean. "Hanging Out: A Research Methodology." *Legacy: A Journal of American Women Writers* 27, no. 1 (2010): 140–159. https://doi.org/10.5250/legacy.27.1.140.

Pitzek, Kristopher. "Copyright Law and the Democraticization of Cultural Value." *Global Societies Journal* 1, no. 1 (2013). https://escholarship.org/uc/item/9dr224z3.

Posner, Richard A. "Legal Pragmatism Defended." *University of Chicago Law Review* 71 (2004): 683–90.

Press, Associated. "5Pointz Graffiti Artists Awarded $6.7m in Lawsuit after Renowned Work Torn Down." *The Guardian*, February 13, 2018, sec. US news. http://www.theguardian.com/us-news/2018/feb/12/graffiti-artists-5pointz-lawsuit.

Rancière, Jacques. *Le partage du sensible: esthétique et politique*. Paris: La Fabrique éd., 2000.

Rao, Sonia. "H&M's Battle with the Artist Revok Shows How Street Art Is Being Taken Seriously." *Washington Post*, March 16, 2018. https://www.washingtonpost.com/news/arts-and-entertainment/wp/2018/03/16/hms-battle-with-the-artist-revok-shows-how-street-art-is-being-taken-seriously/.

Riggle, Nicholas Alden. "Street Art: The Transfiguration of the Commonplaces." *The Journal of Aesthetics and Art Criticism* 68, no. 3 (2010): 243–57.

Riggle, Nicholas Alden. "Using the Street for Art: A Reply to Baldini." *The Journal of Aesthetics and Art Criticism* 74, no. 2 (2016): 191–95. https://doi.org/10.1111/jaac.12280.

Rivasi, Pietro. *1984: Evoluzione e Rigenerazione Del Writing*. Modena: Galleria Civica di Modena, 2016.

Rivasi, Pietro. "Vandalism as Art: Unauthorized Paintings Vs Institutional Art Shows and Events – the Modena Case Study." In *Un(Authorized)//Commissioned*, by Pietro Rivasi and Andrea Baldini, 11–15. Rome: Whole Train Press, 2018.

Rivasi, Pietro, and Andrea Baldini. *Un(Authorized)//Commissioned*. Rome: Whole Train Press, 2018.

Rosner, Elizabeth, and Natalie O'Neill. "Accused Subway Vandal Arrested Again as He Leaves Court." *New York Post* (blog), April 23, 2018. https://nypost.com/2018/04/23/accused-subway-vandal-arrested-again-as-he-leaves-court/.

Rotondi, Gianluca. "Il giudice e la multa ad Alicè « La sua arte non basta »." *Corriere Di Bologna*, February 26, 2016. http://corrieredibologna.corriere.it/bologna/notizie/cronaca/2016/26-febbraio-2016/giudice-multa-ad-alice-la-sua-arte-non-basta-24099108117.shtml.

Salib, Peter N. "The Law of Banksy: Who Owns Street Art?" *The University of Chicago Law Review* 82, no. 4 (2015): 2293–2328.

Saul, Emily. "Subway Vandals from Spain Avoid Jail for Graffiti Spree." *New York Post* (blog), June 14, 2018. https://nypost.com/2018/06/13/subway-vandals-from-spain-avoid-jail-for-graffiti-spree/.

Schultz, Mark F. "Copynorms: Copyright and Social Norms." SSRN Scholarly Paper. Rochester, NY: Social Science Research Network, 2006. https://papers.ssrn.com/abstract=933656.

Senie, Harriet F. "Richard Serra's 'Tilted Arc': Art and Non-Art Issues." *Art Journal* 48, no. 4 (1989): 298–392.

Senie, Harriet F. *The Tilted Arc Controversy: Dangerous Precedent?* Ann Arbor, MI: University of Minnesota Press, 2002.

Serra, Richard. "Art and Censorship." *Nova Law Review* 14, no. 2 (1990): 323–32.

Serra, Richard. "Art and Censorship." *Critical Inquiry* 17, no. 3 (1991): 574–81.

Serra, Richard. "Tilted Arc Destroyed." *Art in America* 77 (1989): 34–47.

Serra, Richard. "Tilted Arc Destroyed." *Nova Law Review* 14, no. 2 (1990): 385–406.

Simoes, Patricia. "Vespa Ads Not Cool." *Spacing Toronto* (blog). Accessed May 30, 2015. http://spacing.ca/toronto/2008/04/30/vespa-ads-not-cool/.

"Slow Food Presidia – What We Do." *Slow Food Foundation* (blog). Accessed August 6, 2018. https://www.fondazioneslowfood.com/en/what-we-do/slow-food-presidia/.

Snyder, Gregory J. *Graffiti Lives: Beyond the Tag in New York's Urban Underground*. New York: New York University Press, 2009.

Summers, Robert. "How Law Is Formal and Why It Matters." *Cornell Law Review* 82 (1997): 1165–1229.

Summers, Robert. "The Formal Character of Law." *The Cambridge Law Journal* 51, no. 2 (1992): 242–62.

Sveinsdóttir, Ásta Kristjana. "Essentiality Conferred." *Philosophical Studies* 140, no. 1 (2008): 135–48. https://doi.org/10.1007/s11098-008-9230-4.

Sveinsdóttir, Ásta Kristjana. "Siding with Euthyphro: Response-Dependence and Conferred Properties." *European Journal of Philosophy* 18, no. 1 (2010): 108–25. https://doi.org/10.1111/j.1468-0378.2008.00303.x.

Sveinsdóttir, Ásta Kristjana. "The Social Construction of Human Kinds." *Hypatia* 28, no. 4 (2013): 716–32. https://doi.org/10.1111/j.1527-2001.2012.01317.x.

"The History of Street Art." *Widewalls*. Accessed September 20, 2018. https://www.widewalls.ch/the-history-of-street-art.

"The Met Says 'Suggestive' Balthus Painting Will Stay After Petition for Its Removal Is Signed by Thousands." *artnet News*, December 5, 2017. https://news.artnet.com/art-world/met-museum-responds-to-petition-calling-for-removal-of-balthus-painting-1169105.

"The Words: Graffiti Glossary." Accessed June 22, 2016. https://www.graffiti.org/faq/graffiti.glossary.html.

Thibault, Ally. "Beijing's Thriving Graffiti Culture May Surprise You." *Public Radio International*. Accessed May 25, 2015. http://www.pri.org/stories/2014-04-21/beijings-thriving-graffiti-culture-may-surprise-you.

"Thinking About the Origins of Street Art, Part 1." *Hyperallergic*, December 16, 2010. https://hyperallergic.com/14166/origins-of-street-art/.

"UPDATE: Artists Revok, Reyes and Steel Are Suing Roberto Cavalli for Copyright Infringement." *HYPEBEAST*. Accessed May 1, 2018. https://hypebeast.com/2015/2/artists-revok-reyes-and-steel-are-suing-roberto-cavalli-for-copyright-infringement.

Vaidhyanathan, Siva. *Copyrights and Copywrongs: The Rise of Intellectual Property and How It Threatens Creativity*. New York: New York University Press, 2001.

Valjakka, Minna. "Graffiti in China – Chinese Graffiti?" *The Copenhagen Journal of Asian Studies* 29, no. 1 (2011): 61–91.

Vartanian, Hrag. "Street Art Politics & Commercialization … How Far Is Too Far?" *Hyperallergic*. Accessed May 30, 2015. http://hyperallergic.com/3415/street-art-politics-commercialization/.

"Vespa Murketing Inspires Fauxreel Backlash?" Accessed May 30, 2015. http://www.murketing.com/journal/?p=1310.

Vimercati, Giovanni. "Blu v Bologna: New Shades of Grey in the Street Art Debate." *The Guardian*, March 17, 2016. http://www.theguardian.com/artanddesign/2016/mar/17/street-artist-blu-destroys-murals-in-bologna.

Walmsley, Ben. "Deep Hanging out in the Arts: An Anthropological Approach to Capturing Cultural Value." *International Journal of Cultural Policy* 24, no. 2 (2018): 272–91. https://doi.org/10.1080/10286632.2016.1153081.

Weaver, Timothy. "The Privatization of Public Space: The New Enclosures." SSRN Scholarly Paper. Rochester, NY: Social Science Research Network, 2014. http://papers.ssrn.com/abstract=2454138.

Weinrib, Ernest J. "Legal Formalism." In *A Companion to Philosophy of Law and Legal Theory*, 327–38. Malden, MA and Oxford, UK: Wiley-Blackwell, 2010. https://doi.org/10.1002/9781444320114.ch20.

Wittgenstein, Ludwig. *Philosophical Investigations*. Oxford, UK: Blackwell, 1953.

Wollheim, Richard. *Art and Its Objects*. Cambridge, UK: Cambridge University Press, 1980.

Wollheim, Richard. *Painting as an Art*. Princeton: Princeton University Press, 1987.

Woods, Amanda, Priscilla DeGregory, and Ruth Brown. "Interpol Helps NYPD Catch Subway Graffiti Artists." *New York Post* (blog), April 20, 2018. https://nypost.com/2018/04/20/interpol-helps-nypd-catch-subway-graffiti-artists/.

Young, Alison. *Street Art, Public City: Law, Crime and the Urban Imagination*. Abingdon, Oxon; New York, NY: Routledge, 2014.

Zuidervaart, Lambert. *Art in Public: Politics, Economics, and a Democratic Culture*. New York, NY: Cambridge University Press, 2011.

www.ingramcontent.com/pod-product-compliance
Lightning Source LLC
Chambersburg PA
CBHW071353230926
51846CB00002B/543
*9789004394032*